PATH
WITHOUT
FORM

Other books by Robert Powell:

Zen and Reality
Crisis in Consciousness
J. Krishnamurti—The Man and His Teaching
The Free Mind
Return to Meaningfulness
The Great Awakening
The Wisdom of Sri Nisargadatta Maharaj
The Ultimate Medicine (Editor)
The Nectar of Immortality (Editor)
The Experience of Nothingness (Editor)
Dialogues on Reality
Discovering the Realm Beyond Experience

PATH WITHOUT FORM

A Journey into the Realm Beyond Thought

A Revised and Expanded Edition of
Why Does God Allow Suffering?

by *Robert Powell, Ph.D.*

BLUE DOVE PRESS
SAN DIEGO • CALIFORNIA
1999

Other Robert Powell books from Blue Dove Press

The Ultimate Medicine
The Nectar of Immortality
The Experience of Nothingness
Dialogues on Reality
Discovering the Realm Beyond Appearance

Blue Dove Press publishes and distributes books by and about sages and saints of all religions as well as other inspiring works. Catalog sent free upon request. Write to:

Blue Dove Press
4204 Sorrento Valley Blvd., Suite K
San Diego, CA 92121
Phone: (619) 623-3330 or 800-691-1008
E-mail: bdp@bluedove.com
website: www.bluedove.com

FIRST EDITION

Cover and text design:
Brian Moucka, Poppy Graphics, Santa Barbara, California

Original cover art by Tracy Dezenzo

ISBN: 1-884997-21-X
Printed in Canada

Library Cataloging-in-Publication Data:
Powell,Robert, 1918-
Path without Form: a journey into the realm beyond
thought/
by Robert Powell.--1st American edition
     p.   cm.
Rev. and expanded ed. of: Why does God allow suffering?
1989.
ISBN 1-884997-21-X (perfect bound)
1. Spiritual life. 'I. Powell, Robert, 1918- Why does
God allow suffering? II. Title.
BL624.P68 1999
291.2--dc21   98-47967
                                             CIP

ABOUT THE AUTHOR

ROBERT POWELL was born in Amsterdam in 1918. After obtaining his doctorate in chemistry from London University, he pursued a career first as an industrial chemist and later as a science writer and editor in Britain and the United States. In 1968 and 1969, he published nine chemical engineering monographs in use by academic and industrial libraries throughout the world.

Robert Powell's personal exploration of spirituality began in the 1960's, and led him to study Zen and a number of spiritual masters including J. Krishnamurti and Ramana Maharshi. His own spiritual awakening coincided with his discovery of the teachings of Sri Nisargadatta Maharaj. He is the editor of a Nisargadatta trilogy, also published by Blue Dove Press, as well as the author of a number of books on what he describes as "human consciousness transformation." Powell lives a busy life with his wife, Gina, in La Jolla, California.

"If the doors of perception were cleansed, everything would appear to man as it is, infinite..."

—William Blake

CONTENTS

Introduction   *ix*

PART ONE

1. Truth Seeker   3
2. The Primal Delusion   7
3. Freedom from the Known   13
4. The Fragmentary and the Holistic Approach towards Understanding   17
5. Where to Start in the Spiritual Life?   21
6. Roots   27
7. The Numbers Game   33
8. The Numbers Game (2)   37
9. On the Importance of Self-Esteem   41
10. "When Does Life Begin?"   45
11. Work Within the System, or Without?   49
12. No More Violent Confrontations   53
13. Has Man a Future?   57
14. The Golden Rule   61
15. "The High I.Q.'s Shall Inherit the Earth"   63
16. Negative Imagination   67
17. Why Does God Allow Suffering?   71
18. The Pleasure Trap   75
19. Just One Little Thing   81

Part Two

20. Morality and Spirituality   87
21. Some Observations on Upanishads   91
    and Early Greek Thought
22. Birthless and Deathless   99
23. Who Am I?—The Impossible Question   101
24. Clearing the Semantic Fog Around Our Self 105
25. From Thought to Insight: 113
    An Unbridgeable Gap
26. The Razor-Edged Path   121
27. A New Approach to an Old Problem   129
28. Seeing Through Oneself   135
29. To Freeze or Not to Freeze,   143
    That is the Question—Or is It?
30. The Discovery of Immortality   151
31. The Observer is the Observed   157
32. Eternity is Ever Now   167
33. Life, Death, and Reincarnation   171
34. Man, a Self-Determined and   175
    Self-Conditioned Entity
35. The Ultimate Transcendence of   179
    the Body-Mind System
36. Know Your Beginning   185
37. About the Reality or Unreality of Reality   189
38. *Advaita* (Non-Duality) —   195
    The Ultimate Teaching
39. A Turned-Around Life   199
40. Questions and Answers   203
41. Probings   221

INTRODUCTION

These essays and shorter pieces of writing were produced over a period of almost thirty years. Some of them are outward-looking, dealing with events of the day (Part One); others are inward-looking, in a meditative sense, and are somewhat more technical in their treatment of the subject (Part Two). This division is basically for the convenience of the reader, for ultimately the outer and the inner are one. Yet, at the same time, the sequence of the material in the book reflects somewhat the way I have developed spiritually, if not in the nature of my understanding, then in depth of insight.

Initially, my vision and writings were strongly influenced by J. Krishnamurti and his mode of expression, and this is apparent in Part One. Later, as I sought to deepen and broaden my understanding, I found the teachings of two modern Indian sages, Sri Ramana Maharshi and Sri Nisargadatta Maharaj, who each express the traditional Upanishadic lore in their own uniquely creative way, extremely helpful. There were also many meeting points with that which I already had discovered on my own. In view of Krishnamurti's total rejection of the traditional wisdom, the reader may wonder whether this indicates a change in spiritual orientation, or even a regression, on my part. No, it does not. More accurately, it may be said to represent a change in scope and perspective.

Krishnamurti's teaching, in my view, is essentially a psychological teaching; it is concerned with the psyche as distinct from the material world. His primary thrust is to expose our conflict-ridden mind, to clear it of all forms of conditioning through a process that he calls "choiceless awareness." He never ceases to stress the necessity for a total transformation in consciousness, in order to create a better world. The teaching has the virtue of simplicity and, if understood correctly, may lead to a realization of the state of Non-Duality or *Advaita* that is the very goal of the Upanishadic Masters. Yet, philosophically speaking, my scientific curiosity never felt completely satisfied. There still seemed to remain a subtle form of duality between body and mind, matter and spirit. In my own explorations, I had already perceived the unreality of such divisions, and I found the same unified vision in the Maharshi and later when I came upon Nisargadatta. Also, I noticed that there was much less emphasis, less missionary zeal as it were, on improving the world and more on living with the existing order, since in the end, all that is illusory anyway and the only thing that is truly Real and matters is one's Self, which is perfect the way it is. Also, once one has realized the illusion of separateness and the non-existence of a "doer," who is there to transform the consciousness and affect the world? And what is the entity whose consciousness needs to be transformed? In Krishnamurti, despite his statement "You are the world," one misses recognition of the latter element since he does not acknowledge the existence of *Maya* or Illusion as a veil, or superimposition, on the Self. Nisargadatta once stated that even if a perfect society were theoretically possible, it would not be durable since such a society would be utterly unstable.

So much for my own journey of discovery. At this stage, a few words may perhaps be said of general interest to the spiritual aspirant. First, I have found that people are confused as to which of the many possible approaches to spirituality to select and also where and how to start. But the fact of the matter is that Truth cannot be given to one by anyone else, not even by the greatest Master, as all the enlightened sages have testified. Only by turning within, or by self-enquiry, can anything of value be discovered and made one's own. And truly great discoveries await the one who is sufficiently motivated by his love for such self-inquiry! Any authentically acquired insight can then be the starting point for an ever-deepening exploration, for only through proper understanding of what one is can deliverance be brought about from all that which binds us. In this process, the external teacher can function only as a catalyst; that is, he can lead us to the well but cannot make us drink the clear waters of what is.

The reader may further ask: Are there then no fundamental differences among the various teachers? The question is particularly pertinent, since the novice today is faced with a bewildering choice of teachings, gurus and spiritual movements. My answer to this is that there are both differences and there is no difference. There is no difference in the sense that all enlightened sages are speaking from the same standpoint, that of the Absolute, which cannot be expressed by any means. (If their wisdom does not well up from the Ultimate but from the body-mind level, then their pronouncements are not spiritual truth at all but more properly belong to the realm of philosophy or psychology.) And the differences are only in their approach to that ineffable Truth; there are an almost unlimited number of ways of approaching the subject and each Master has his own unique way of doing so. To prevent further confusion, I hasten to add that by the term "approach" I do not mean a "path" as commonly understood; that is, a methodology or technique with a fixed set of "do's" and "don'ts," to be executed over a period of time. By "approach" I mean more a way of looking at the problem of man's predicament, which implies the choice of a verbal framework to describe it—a kind of spiritual diagnosis—whereby the "prescription" already lies within the diagnosis. The approaches can be manifold, but the "therapeutic event" or spiritual catharsis is ever the same in nature as well as end result.

Then, one may ask: Which particular Master can be recommended to the novice as providing the most direct and fruitful avenue? If I were to advise anyone, I would say follow that Master whose approach is the most congenial to you, the most compatible with your own temperament and inclinations. It is a purely individual decision. Nisargadatta, when asked the question, How do I decide as to who is the best guru for me?, suggested to accept one meaningful pronouncement of any guru who appeals to one. Take that pronouncement fully to heart and have trust in your own self, your own consciousness, who is your ultimate true guru (from an unpublished talk in Bombay, 1980). All correct approaches lead to the same goal, so once one has made a choice in this respect, it is important only to stick with the enquiry and apply oneself to its pursuit with total honesty and determination. Then, after having done this for some time, one may find that there are other approaches as well which can be equally helpful and lead to the same ultimate insights.

On the following pages, I have recorded some of my adventures in self-exploration, milestones on the path of deliverance, and hope they may be of some help to others in their own emancipation.

PATH
WITHOUT
FORM

PART ONE

1

TRUTH SEEKER

The seeker after Absolute Truth
finds himself in a mansion of indefinite dimension.
To proceed in the search,
he must open the door that leads to the treasure.
But lo and behold, upon doing so,
he finds only another door that leads to the goal.
So on this journey the seeker opens many doors
and everlastingly finds, not absolute truth,
but another step to take, through another door to go
to the sanctum of Truth.
After thusly pursuing many truths,
each pointing to, and leaning upon another truth,
all in the relative sphere and thus not the Absolute,
which depends only on itself
because it just is,
our seeker suddenly comes to a halt
in order to take stock of his search.

He looks before him and knows
there is an infinite regress of portals to Truth.
He looks behind him and knows there is
an infinite regress of entrances toward Absolute Truth.
And he knows he may travel in either direction,
but it will be to no avail,
because the journey is infinite in duration:
ever seeking, ever traveling, never finding, never arriving.
All that he will encounter on this journey will be
little truths that cannot stand on their own
because they are ever supported
by other little truths
that, in turn, rest on still others,
and so on, ad infinitum.

So our weary voyager after Truth is paralyzed in his resolve.
He realizes that whatever move he makes will be energy wasted,
staying on the periphery of the circle that surrounds the kernel
which is Truth, but never approaching.
He clearly sees he will never attain the goal,
as long as he futilely enters doorway after doorway —
which is the endless process of information gathering and
cultivation of memory,
wherein the resulting vision will ever remain fragmentary,
never complete.
He is rooted on the spot without the slightest move,
for he knows not how to proceed, is in total paralysis.
Yet he knows one thing now with absolute certainty:

Truth is not to be found on this sojourn—
he must forget his search, on those lines as anticipated.

And in the very stillness of his not-knowing,
of awaiting the answer, how to proceed,
suddenly, in his mind's eye,
he sees the entire mansion of knowledge
as being of infinite dimension, of Maya *without limits;*
that is, without answers that satisfy and sustain.
For a split second he feels the floor under his feet has vanished,
he is floating in space, the Emptiness
surrounds him and even penetrates him . . .
Gone are all fixed values, part of tradition.
All certainties are false, man-made through insecurity,
mere moral crutches.
No satisfaction is lasting, essentially momentary,
a fleeting thought.
All is indeterminate, relative, in a flux, including the seeker's self
who is now perceived as no different from that
which he so eagerly sought.
For Truth's pilgrim, the mansion no longer even exists,
and at that very moment,
he is the Truth....

2 ~

THE PRIMAL DELUSION

Could it be that at the root of the human predicament lies a basic truth about ourselves, the non-recognition of which is the ultimate cause of all unhappiness? This writer thinks so. Inherent to the human condition is this susceptibility to anxiety, frustration, exasperation — all those painful intrusions which never seem to leave the mind alone for very long. We have so many explanations for what ails us: lack of security, an unhappy childhood haunting us up to our present days, loneliness, and so forth; but it seems to me that although these terms describe very real states of mind, they are still on the level of symptoms and there is something amiss on a much deeper level. A real "sickness of the 'soul'" exists — if I may put it thus metaphorically albeit somewhat inaccurately — which gives rise to all suffering.

Since the understanding of the root cause may go some way in relieving our distress, it may be worthwhile to sketch very briefly the situation confronting the human psyche. Man is born out of non-duality, out of the Void, a blob of nothingness, as it were, into a world that emphasizes "thingness" and "selfhood" — implying essentially "separateness." He is life, but through living in the world, through education, through conditioning, this life is soon whittled down, restricted — all this being an inevitable side effect of the crystallization of the ego in a culture that has lost all contact with Reality. Exhorted to "look out for himself," to "get on in the world," the individual from his earliest youth becomes a "competitor"; then, as time goes by, he gets increasingly isolated from his fellow beings and cut off from the source of his being.

Thus the primary duality is brought about: What man basically is — part of Life in which there is absolutely no place for any form of psychological security, for this would entail a separate and enduring entity — and what man is led to believe he is: something of importance that, in a process of "growth" or "evolution," is going to be more and more "established" in life. The latter ideation comes about through the particular form of cultivation of the mind which results from the entire cultural process.

On the material level, we surround ourselves with so many things, which become something like indispensable to us. We cling to these material possessions because their continuous presence strengthens the illusion of our own continuity, which underlies the fallacious idea of a more or less permanent "self." Hence, anything at all familiar in our perceptive life is deeply reassuring (but reassuring of "what"?) Second, material possessions, through their value as status symbols, are highly effective in fostering our feelings of self-importance and security — the comfort-giving thoughts that we like to fall back upon whenever the realization of our essential poverty of spirit and general inadequacy becomes too hard to bear.

Intellectually, it is the same story. It is not the intellectual activities *per se* that matter to any great extent, but primarily their achievement-value and recognition in society. The more they build us up, naturally, the more vulnerable we are to a reversal of the process.

Religiously, too, it can be seen that the organized religions, each in its own way, aim at giving sustenance and solace to our illusory existence, with promises of rewards in a hypothetical life hereafter and other "goodies" obtainable only if we conform to certain kinds of behavior prescribed by our saviors as "virtue."

Now, surveying this whole sorry picture of self-deception in its various manifestations, it may perhaps be asked: What is so wrong with a harmless delusion? Why cannot the mind believe in something, even if it is actually a complete mirage? The answer to this must be that inherently there is nothing "bad" or "good" in make-believe; only that as soon as this make-believe proceeds beyond the point of no return — that is, where it can no longer be recognized as such — man is at once extremely vulnerable. For then his whole complicated existence is at stake; he may well lose all that he has fought for so bitterly over the years. Essentially, all mental anguish and suffering spring from this non-recognition of the basic duality of our state of being: this is the primal delusion.

On the other hand, that rare man who has not the slightest illusion about himself and his position in the world, because he knows what he is — absolutely nothing — is not vulnerable at all. Nothing can be taken away from him, because he possesses nothing. All that he appears to own, he merely holds in trust. He is Life, and can Life be detracted from? Because such existence is timeless, he is not even touched by death.

So, we can now recognize the following situation. Man, once he is conditioned to believe in his separate identity, is not only isolated from his fellow beings — and this must inevitably be so as long as the degree of success obtained in the competitive struggle for (psychological) survival is essentially the basis for what is considered to be "happiness" — but he is also isolated from the possibility of ever going back to that state of pristine purity which prevailed before his emergence from the Void. He cannot possibly go back to that, yet there is always consciously, and more so unconsciously, a nostalgic desire for this state of unification: the urge to return to the womb, as it were. Does this not lie at the root of so many of our social and personal strivings: the effort to "belong" somewhere, to find a niche in life where one is not too much noticed, to find fulfillment in love, the desire to have many hours of blissful sleep without dreams — all these indicating the longing to merge oneself with something other or greater than self? In this way, the mind seeks to counterbalance the brutal and relentless drive to maintain and foster its "individuality," at the same time making man forget that essentially he is frightened, alone, vulnerable, void.

3 &

FREEDOM FROM
THE KNOWN

The typical intellectual, especially in the West, expects clear-cut answers to the great philosophical questions of all time. But the really fundamental issues in life cannot be meaningfully viewed in terms of black and white, and perhaps not even in shades of gray. For this is essentially the way of the computer, functioning rigidly within a binary system; and no computer program can reflect more than a small fragment of reality.

Man, however, has the capacity to transcend the limitations of his dualistic upbringing, which has resulted in the discursive intellect. To do this, he must go beyond all computer language, beyond the arbitrary semantic parameters which form the atoms of his thought-world.

One of the most glaring examples of the inadequacy of the traditional approach to philosophical problems is the age-old free will-predestination controversy. If one looks at this problem in terms of "either/or," there never is a solution, because whatever answer one comes up with can always be controverted by further argument. But if one begins the inquiry by searching for meaning in one's very terms of reference, one arrives at a paradoxical situation in which it is seen that both sides of the argument have validity, yet are not mutually exclusive. There is the ubiquitous law of cause and effect, the cornerstone of determinism; but there is also a universal intelligence, which, once awakened, is free to discover the truth of causality. The seeing of causality as a fact in, for example, the development of the acorn into oak tree, does not rest on opinion, belief, desire, and is therefore unconditioned; thus, the operation of this intelligence is no part of causality.

The human mind evinces this paradox strikingly, alternating rare flashes of insight into what *is* — which are moments of absolute freedom — with long periods of cerebration (the human computer at work!), in which it is continually activated by the emotional scars of past experiences and is therefore totally in bondage. One can also make the ironical observation that man can be very creative, very inventive, with regard to mechanical things; but when it comes to his own psyche, he generally is highly mechanical, apathetic, and virtually completely unaware. And when the psyche is unfree, functioning like a machine, any creativity that man is capable of is essentially corrupted and to no avail in his search for happiness.

In this writer's view, mankind's present psychological condition makes liberation, in the deepest sense of the word, an impossibility. No amount of Yoga, "meditation" or other so-called spiritual practices can buy freedom for man, so long as his mind remains a conditioned entity whose functioning is entirely predetermined. Nevertheless, there is a glimmer of hope, but only if man can bring himself to change fundamentally on all levels of his being. Such a change would only come out of a revolutionary conception of the "me," springing from a direct seeing, leading to the relinquishment of all aspirations for the "progress" of that "me" in the world — for it is these very aspirations that form our shackles. Now this final renunciation is a ruthless business — a kind of dying — involving the shattering of all our "dreams" and of the various images of self which we cultivate so assiduously. Few people are ready for this or willing to go through with it; some still think in terms of compromise, as though such a thing were possible.

An unprecedented reorientation of this nature would have to go hand in hand with new thinking on other fundamental issues, such as life and death, "purpose" in an individual's life and in the Universe, and the meaning of Time — issues which are really part and parcel of the problem of the self. This new thinking will have to proceed not so much from what we already "know," which is largely a collection of folklore designed to induce euphoria, but from what we do not know but have the capacity to find out through observation and reflection. In this search, there really is only one obstacle, and that is man's fear of the unknown. Because man clings unthinkingly to the known, which to him spells security, he blocks himself in his search for freedom, remaining, in effect, a prisoner of his own ideologies.

4

The Fragmentary and the Holistic Approach towards Understanding

Historically, most approaches towards a better understanding of man and the universe have been pursued within more or less well defined scholastic areas, with as yet little liaison or contact between them. In more recent times, with the advent of the era of the specialist, this trend has become even more pronounced. Science, philosophy, medicine and psychology carry on merrily in their respective courses, without much regard for any unity underlying all knowledge. Thus, each is developing within a watertight compartment, with its own language or jargon that is often not even understood by any of the other disciplines, and each having its own methodology in probing the unknown.

Now it seems to me that specialization in any field inevitably introduces limitation and some distortion of the truth, not only because specialists usually end up by "knowing almost everything about almost nothing," as the saying goes, and therefore what they know is hardly worth knowing, but also because, in the very process of specialization, something in the overall picture gets lost that is very essential to man's understanding. Each of the existing approaches being inherently fragmentary, the end result must necessarily be of a like nature. In other words, the integration of a great deal of fragmentary information does not always add up to a reliable or accurate picture of the Whole; or, as it has been summarized: the Whole is more than the sum total of its parts!

Is a reverse approach possible, an approach that starts with an examination of man's entire existence and then fills out the picture by studying the various details? Recently, with the realization of the close interrelationship of body and mind, there has been a certain rapprochement between medicine and psychology, leading to the new branch of psychosomatic medicine; but this is an as yet relatively rare example of what can be achieved through the building of bridges between various disciplines. And even here we are some way yet from the total acceptance of non-duality, which does not recognize any absolute divisions between mind and matter, between the material world and the biological world, between one individual and another, and so on.

To this writer, there exists an altogether different approach towards knowledge and insight. It is not a novel approach, having been known in some areas of the world for thousands of years, but is presently largely anathema to orthodox learning. It takes as its point of departure the entire field of experiential existence, the whole of consciousness. In this attack on the unknown, one ruthlessly refuses to be sidetracked by detail, by assumptions or speculation, by knowledge — and, inherently, all knowledge is partial or fragmentary — but one comes to an integral understanding by a very close examination, coupled with extensive explorative contemplation, of a very few pertinent facts. Because the investigation is in depth, penetrating to the very foundation of our knowing and thinking, and thereby contacting the non-dualistic substratum of all manifestation, it does not become yet another form of specialization. Such an exploration must necessarily lead to the realization of the Emptiness or Unmanifested that underlies all existence and which, being the source of everything, unites the various disparate aspects of our existence. This will not only put an end to all doubts, but also open up an entirely unexpected vista of tremendous magnitude and beauty, making our vision truly whole.

Once having seen the great truth of non-duality, it will then be possible to return to the various individual branches of learning with greatly enhanced understanding, and to work within the artificial barriers separating the various disciplines and yet not be hampered by them in any way. One might call this "to work within the system and yet not be of it."

5

WHERE TO START
IN THE SPIRITUAL LIFE?

We talk glibly about the need for a more "spiritual" orientation in life. But what is really meant by that? The word "spiritual" is difficult to define, because our ordinary experience does not touch it. Spirituality has nothing to do with doctrine, beliefs, so-called spiritual practice, or with systems of philosophy. A spiritual life does not consist in talking endlessly about Reality, but in getting a taste of it — just like reading a menu is not the same as dining. The nearest to indicate its meaning is to say that it begins with self-knowing, with being aware of one's thoughts, desires, fears, motivations — in short, the whole machinery of the mind.

What are the essential qualifications for such an orientation? First, honesty — total honesty with oneself, if not with others. Second, inquisitiveness, a true spirit of inquiry. Why take an interest only in *outer* space — which is the "world" — as we all do, and not in *inner* space, which is oneself? This then is the way to start. And if one does, one finds there is a movement taking place, one is on a journey — an endless venture. And the farther one travels, the more one comes into a new and vibrant type of energy. It is this energy that is going to be the transforming factor. We must, however, surrender ourselves totally to that energy for the miracle to take place.

Third, there must be an urgency for knowing self, because one recognizes the self as the clue to everything else in the Universe. And, especially, because one sees the mischief done through non-investigation, through non-understanding of this mechanism whereby one is always responsible for one's own unhappiness and, by extension, also for the greater sorrow suffered in the world at large. Thus, one perceives the urgent necessity for putting a stop to it, and for this we must find out how the ego ever creates problems in the world.

These three factors, it appears to me, are the essentials for making a start in the spiritual life, for putting one's house in order; and their importance is not necessarily in the order given here. In fact, each factor is as important as the others!

So, if one fits the bill with respect to these requirements, and if one has the necessary urgency to come to grips with one's life — because it is seen to be a meaningless farce as currently lived — then one really starts to learn. This learning is a process that has a beginning but no ending. And if one is lucky enough — there are no guarantees in such matters — one may experience a taste of reality and come to a vision of life that is at once exquisitely beautiful and ludicrously simple. From the conventional point of view, it is also simply ludicrous, because the whole world appears topsy-turvy in every aspect. Furthermore, since the new world view cannot by any stretch of the imagination be reconciled with the generally accepted one — and one must totally reject the latter because of its perceived unreality — one is automatically a revolutionary, and an uncompromising one at that.

Although the discovery that one has made is a personal one, it is not a new discovery for mankind. At least three thousand years ago in India, certain "rishis" (seers) discussed their vision of life with their disciples. These discourses were subsequently recorded in "scriptures" — the Vedas and Upanishads. The Upanishads have been called the most revolutionary teaching extant. And it is precisely because, at first glance, it is so utterly implausible for the uninitiated, that whenever its reality is rediscovered by an individual, it does not meet with a sympathetic response by society, if there is any response at all; nor is it usually connected in people's minds with what is probably mankind's oldest wisdom teaching. The new insights are simply too "far out," too far removed from the range of everyday experience to be seriously considered. Thus, the point is missed completely that it concerns a reconfirmation of the insights divulged and elaborated upon in the various Upanishads.

To live in tune with their truths signifies a "divorce" from life as it is generally being lived, a total disengagement from everything that holds us, limits our inner freedom. For one thing, this means the end of all expectations, both large and small, except on a practical, technological level. Has one ever tried to live without any expectations whatsoever? Then life is totally concentrated in the present moment, with no energy being frittered away in speculating about the future or brooding over the past, "what should or might have been." Such functioning strictly in the "here-and-now" gives one that special kind of energy to learn, and to go on learning. And by "learning" we mean a seeing of the totality of one's existence at each moment, without ever accumulating any information or images into one's memory banks. At first, such seeing without a background, without memories, is sporadic, fairly shallow, and it is easy to slip back toward the level of thought, which is within the movement of time. But if the necessary interest is maintained and so the necessary energy flow, the awareness becomes more intensive and extensive until a point is reached at which one is permanently beyond slipping back. In orthodox Christian terms, one is "saved." But essentially one is no different from what one has always been, except that one has woken up from the deep slumber in the dream world of space and time into the "awakened" state of timeless reality, in which all objects and concepts that previously complicated one's life are seen as an unreal film of events projected by mind-thought. The existence of that film's subjective reality to the "individual" is, however, not denied; it is accepted as a fact of dualistic existence, but it is no longer given objective reality by identification with it: one is merely, and strictly, a witness, the witnessing intelligence. All that happens takes place within that intelligence, but that intelligence itself is subservient to nothing; it is therefore entirely free, and eternally peaceful.

6 〰

Roots

This writer concurs wholeheartedly with the present emphasis on searching for one's roots, except that he suggests doing so radically (after all, "radically" means "of or from the root"). And to radically go back to one's origin means that one searches for one's roots as an *individual* and not just as a member of an ethnic or religious group — which is a very superficial thing. Not that there is anything wrong with the latter; it is just that to do *merely* that has no meaning. It will give the individual some feeling of belonging, which is security to him, and in this way bind him even more strongly to the collective.

To search for one's individual roots means to explore how one has come about as a psychological entity in a world that is essentially non-definable, empty. Thus, the discovery of what one is must mean the very opposite of fostering one's sense of belonging, because it is a return to a state of total aloneness or Nothingness and thereby the destruction of all security.

When one begins to investigate into one's roots as a

person, which is one's identity, one observes at the outset only two basic things: the existence of a body, and an apparently endless stream of thoughts, which we refer to as "the mind."

First, the body. We say it is *my* body, but this is really begging the question, because it presupposes the existence of a "me" that can lay claim to this body — and it is precisely the existence of that "me" which is at issue in this investigation. The body itself does not say "this is 'me' as a body"; it is the mind that assigns the body's identity. But what is the mind? If mind itself has no identity, then it has no power to confer identity, and body is a mere phenomenon. And how does one observe "body"? Does the body observe itself? Of course not; body is only observed, re-cognized by the mind, in the mind. In other words, body is a mental reflection and has no actual existence in itself. So there is only mind — and mind is actually this continuous thought activity.

Having come to the point that the duality of body/thought has resolved itself naturally into the one term, thought, we shall now observe the latter in some more detail. There is then this endless stream of thoughts, produced by an apparently inexhaustible thought-machine. This in itself is one of the most extraordinary phenomena — a kind of perpetual motion machine, for ever spewing forth thoughts, with nary a rest — which is very much taken for granted.

The distinctive feature of thought is that the thought stream *is not just random*. Like a magnetic field of force is oriented around the magnetic poles, so the thought field is oriented around the perceived body. It is a subtle phenomenon, but it lies at the root of all the psyche's, or psychological, activities. To detect this, one needs the compass of awareness: the sensitivity to watch all motivations for our actions, thoughts. Not just being aware of the most obvious desires, such as for power, lust, sex, etc. — which is easy enough. After a while, the gross desires stop, but the subtle ones continue. And it is not easy to be aware of the many very subtle desires the mind harbors, such as for self-assertion, for the status quo — we want to hang on to what we have — and the hundreds of minor ways of self-gratification.

Apart from this characteristic pattern of the thought content, something is known about its *genesis*. Through inner awareness, man has found that thought comes about through experience — but not any old experience, for that matter. Experience that has been incompletely digested leaves a residue in memory, and it is this residue that kindles thought. In this way, thought perpetuates itself. Only total understanding, the going through an experience without holding back, without any reservations, and with a clear mind, can break the chain.

With the exception of thought in the strictly utilitarian, scientific and abstract contexts, all thought — which means all thought having emotional content — is derived in this manner. So any psychological problem, whether actual or potential, ensures its own continuity. Or, one might say, the momentum of psychologically induced thought is self-sustaining and never-ending.

When one observes the prolific nature of the human

mind, its myriads of psychological activities and complexities, one concludes that man must have a great multitude of problems, numerous unresolved experiences. And this is, of course, so, as we know only too well.

Again, analogous to the situation with respect to the body, there is nothing about thought that indicates self-nature. Thought is merely a flux, a stream; it is like a flame — never the same for two moments. It is not a question of "my" thought or "your" thought: there is only thought. To state that a thought is "my" thought because it is centered around "my" body is simply begging the question and engaging in closed-circuit thinking. It is indeed always such closed-circuit thinking that leads us astray and takes us into unreality.

What are we then that is intrinsically us? What are all the things that we have accepted as "given" without even a moment's consideration? Paradoxically qualities such as name, career, social position, etc., are "given" all right, but given by Society, not by Reality and are therefore not inherent. If there is nothing intrinsic that I can call my own, then I am really a mere "phenomenon," with somewhat limited continuity. But that phenomenon is essentially empty. Just as a flame has the appearance of continuity yet has no identity, because it consists of ever new material and therefore is each moment a new flame — so is the mind a kind of flame that is nurtured by a continuous flux of thought. Thus, it is the pattern of thought in relation to the "body" that has created the fundamental schism in consciousness, the birth of the unreal center, the beginning of *Maya*.

To see this completely, thoroughly, only therein lies liberation. The fact is that all our problems occur only because we are deeply, totally involved with thought, that great seductress. One must perceive the terrifying implications of the power, the momentum of thought — and also the simplicity, the beauty of the solution, the ending of sorrow. Fear, hope, all our expectations, are only the many combinations and permutations of thought, within thought.

Now this realization that there is nothing to substantiate the conventional notion of self totally deflates the concept of self-importance. And this cuts the grass right from under our feet, for if we are totally honest with ourselves we will see that all or most of our activities that are not performed out of sheer necessity in the pursuit of food, clothing, and shelter, are ultimately from motives of self-importance. The discovery of our roots has led us to true humbleness. And also, having seen that what I am is not any one thing in particular, or what comes to the same thing, that I am everything, all that exists, throws quite a different light on my feeling of alienation, of separation from the non-self. It means the end of all striving, even for liberation, since I am complete as I am, eternally liberated; the end of all competition, since I recognize I would only be competing with myself, and the end of all ambition since there is really no such thing as "individual" achievement.

7

THE NUMBERS GAME

I wonder whether one realizes to what increasing extent we engage in numbers games of all kinds; that is, consciously or unconsciously, we give tremendous importance to mere quantity — the almighty concept of "Number." This we do at the expense of everything else, and especially quality. One can observe the phenomenon in all walks of life. In business, we see that everything is valued according to the amount of profit that can be produced and nothing else matters. For example, if wars generate booms in the economy, then hooray for war. We are not talking out of our heads, for during the Vietnam era, a representative committee of business leaders came out overwhelmingly in support of the war in Southeast Asia. Also, during a war, any means are considered justified to achieve the end. In the Second World War in

Germany, owners of the firm of Krupp had no compunction in using slave labor in their zest to maximize output of war matériel.

In industry, sheer volume of output is only too often of paramount importance, and quality takes a secondary place. And in its obsession for ever-expanding sales volume, industry has sought not only to satisfy existing demand for its products and services, but also to create a need where none existed before, thus adding to people's psychological dependencies.

In our schools and colleges, we "educate" larger numbers of students than ever, but what we impart to them in a truly educational sense becomes less and less significant. In religion, the number of churches and their worldly possessions have risen fabulously, but their religious activities, in contradistinction to their purely social ones, have lost any meaning they may once have had. Militarily, we can kill to an almost unlimited extent, yet we still accept war as a valid way of life. Certain nations have amassed vast wealth and power; yet it will be found that in these very same countries there is less and less freedom for the individual. On our highways and through the air we transport ever-increasing numbers of people, but, in doing so, conditions in the cities have become more and more adverse to health and comfort. In communications, more and more information channels of greater capacity are opening up, yet it becomes increasingly difficult to establish the truth about anything. And our overvaluation of mere quantity is apparent above all in human lives, where the average life span has been rising steadily, as has also the standard of living measured as Gross National Product, etc., but the overall quality of life appears to be continually on the downgrade.

This devaluation of quality through inflation of secondary, and often false, values expresses itself in many other ways. We are becoming increasingly computerized, digitized and automated; and thereby each of us is reduced to a mere number — a datum in a set of statistics. In politics, we are categorized as belonging to either a "silent majority" or a "vociferous minority," and so on — showing how everything that we evaluate is in terms of numbers, quantities and proportions. This is not the place to pursue the subject any further, but it seems to me that some of this characteristic attitude is spilling over into our approach towards the spiritual life — a life that, if it is truly "spiritual," lies totally beyond space and time, and, therefore, beyond any quantitative assessment or consideration. By inferring the infusion of a quantitative aspect into an area of life that by virtue of its inherent nature can never be quantified, I have the following in mind. In various conversations that I have had with persons from all walks of life, they readily acknowledged the need for a total change of society. Yet, when asked whether they as individuals were doing anything about it, the answer came in the negative; the reason being that there was little point in doing so until it became apparent that the *majority* of people would change their ways — and this, they averred, would never happen.

Now it may well be that they are right in this respect, that the majority of people have not the energy to pull themselves out of their present rut and therefore will never know what it is to really live. Not having an efficient crystal ball, I cannot say what is going to happen and it may also be that society is already too far gone to challenge itself fundamentally and so will continue to decay ever more. But does this mean there is no need or urgency on the part of the individual to transform himself? Leaving aside the notion that for a transformation of society a numerical majority of transformed individuals is mandatory — and we have very good reasons to doubt this assumption — it seems to me that the whole argument is irrelevant to the individual who clearly perceives what is taking place within himself and the world. Seeing that we are all heading for chaos and insanity, his first priority is to set his own house in order, so that he may live supremely in sanity. It is only an unhealthy mind that follows the masses like sheep, even if everything points to their pursuing a course of ultimate destruction. Order, like love, is its own justification. Only when this is felt very strongly will it be possible to bring it about. Real order will never be created because it is advocated to us as being preferable to chaos, or for any other reason. A mind that has lived all its life in disorder and conflict, will — if it is not completely dulled — naturally have the desire, if not potential, to get out of its misery. It does not have to be coaxed, and does not care even if it is a minority of one.

8 ⟿

THE NUMBERS GAME (2)

In the previous chapter, we stated that there are very good reasons to doubt the assumption made by many people that society cannot be transformed until a *majority* of individuals making up that society have undergone some kind of transformation. First, it seems to me that even on the level of logic the argument does not really hold water. It must be painfully obvious that such a stance only perpetuates the *status quo*: that if everyone thinks in this manner, we shall all be waiting for something to happen that by the logic of the situation cannot possibly happen, ever. But I very much question their basic assumption that a majority is necessary. First, on purely empirical grounds. In other areas of human endeavor, we can see that major innovations have always been initiated by individuals or minorities. Even now

37

most things happen not because the majority wish them to be so or think accordingly. Society is what it is on account of fundamental Ignorance, because of a lack of education; but let us remember: the majority are always educated by a minority. And, in this connection, it is important to realize that nowadays we can bring something to the attention of large numbers of people more quickly and more effectively through our vastly improved means of communication. And although these are used at present largely to brainwash us in every possible way, it must be remembered that they also hold the potential to spread enlightenment. A heartening example is that a man like J. Krishnamurti has been made accessible to millions by radio and television.

A further factor is that the confusion in the world is becoming so apparent and, at times, so disruptive to one's everyday life, that even some of those who are totally engrossed in worldly things are waking up to it; and this may well be a first step towards their self-awareness.

Why do we adopt this attitude of postponement, of want of attention that would bring its own appropriate action, when everyone can see that the house is on fire? It seems to me not only a question of faulty logic, but basically a situation brought about for lack of understanding as to what it is all about; we rationalize, postpone as we evade the issue.

Although we have countered the argument as to a majority being necessary on logical grounds and therefore dualistically, I feel that in this matter both argument and counter-argument — although having validity on a certain level — do not really touch the central issue. To me the issue is that consciousness is not just the summation of the consciousnesses of a number of individual minds. In actual fact, the individual minds have no real, independent existence but it is our delusion that they have. Each individual *is* at once the Collective, the consciousness of the world. To put it somewhat differently, there is only this (collective) consciousness and the concept of "individual" consciousness has come about through a complex mechanism involving various identification processes.

This aspect of reality — that of its fundamental nonduality — is perhaps one of the most difficult to understand. Yet, if it can be seen to be so, it then follows immediately that in applying such quantitative concepts as the "majority" and "minority" we are barking up the wrong tree. Our whole approach was based upon a fallacy; that of thought, which is inherently fragmentary, trying to grasp the Ultimate, which is non-dual and therefore beyond all numbers games — and, in so doing, reduces it to its own level. Therefore, all of its conclusions and explanations are devoid of validity.

9

ON THE IMPORTANCE OF SELF-ESTEEM

Psychologists as well as certain religious movements tell us that when man "suffers" from low self-esteem, he is not likely to achieve happiness and spiritual emancipation.

Are they right? Yes, they are right — but only half. And in that, they are really right for the wrong reason. For them the emphasis is on "low," for us it lies on "self-esteem." A man who has high self-esteem, does he not suffer equally? Of course, although socially he may be somewhat better adjusted, have some more worldly confidence, spiritually — that is, actually — he is no different; he is in no way better off than the person with low self-esteem. Maybe, he is even worse off, for his better adjustment may more easily fool him as to the sickness of society and, consequently, his own sickness.

Would a person with a "middling" degree of self-esteem then be the most advanced and the most likely to achieve happiness? To pursue such a line of reasoning is to see at once its absurdity. First, which self does one evaluate? Like the fragmented beings that we are, there is a multitude of selves in each individual, all clamoring for their right to exist. As long as man is not whole, there is this division as man the father, the husband, the bachelor, the lover, the businessman, the professional, the patriot, the revolutionary, the religionist, the mystic, the spiritual aspirant, the rationalist, and the manifold other roles with which he identifies himself.

Secondly, how does one measure self-esteem, what are one's yardsticks? Is this perhaps another instance of the numbers game man plays with himself, consciously or unconsciously? There is obviously a deep desire to know where one stands on the human scale, as though one's life depends on it. See how many people in this world suffer from inferiority feelings and complexes!

But, before pursuing the matter further: What is the connection between self-esteem and "happiness"? In this respect, what is one's definition of "happiness" — and we must have such a definition before we can attempt to correlate happiness with self-esteem. The many psychologists who constantly espouse the importance of self-esteem for happiness leave us in mid-air just about there. They do not or cannot come up with a mechanism to elucidate such a correlation.

Self-esteem is, of course, a societal concept, because our entire upbringing has been based on comparison.

Competition, ambition, success, riches — these are all quantitative values that make for an esteemed "self." Without the continuous feedback from society, which molds our thoughts and actions, is there a self at all? There is a Self, but it is an Emptiness, a vastness beyond every form of definition or quantification. And that Self has within itself everything — happiness, unhappiness, success, failure — as pairs of opposites and not as single terms that ever strive to attain their counterpart, like the "sinner" trying to become pious, the wicked virtuous, the stupid smart, and so forth. Hence, this Self is in itself free from conflict, eternally tranquil, fulfilled, unaffected, uncorrupted by events. It is whole, and therefore it is blissful. By the same token, he who measures himself in order to raise his self-esteem, in order to complete himself, is still caught up in what the Eastern world calls *Maya* (Sanskrit for "that which is to be measured"). For one thing, self-esteem evaluation ever leads to fear — the fear of not coming up to one's self-projected ideal of self-worth. For another, one remains entangled in the world of limitation — within the world of the little self — and so will never be able to experience the ecstasy of real Happiness.

10

"When Does Life Begin?"

We hear much discussion these days as to what is the exact moment that life commences — whether it is at conception, some time during the fetus stage, or at birth. The argument is typical of our confused notions about what we really are. The answer to the question is, of course: None of the above. Life just *is*: that is, it is indestructible, it does not need initiation, nor can it be diminished by any means.

We identify with the body, and because body appears and disappears, we speculate about the beginning and ending of life. But life is a much greater thing than the appearance or disappearance of a body; it is something much more significant, much deeper than a mere physical appearance, just like death is a much more significant affair than a mere disappearance.

So let the experts — scientific, medical, and legal— deliberate in solemn voices about this "conundrum": they are seeking footprints in the sky. Life has neither beginning nor end, and it will forever escape destruction, definition, and, therefore, delimitation.

Man has it not within his power to kill life, he is neither creator nor destroyer in the absolute sense. Man has it in his power only to create images, and through these images to create great suffering.

So what is important is not life's beginning, but to observe the beginning, the birth of the image which causes so much mischief. Man, the image-maker, is ever violent because essentially the image-making process is a dissection, a cutting-up of what is whole. The primordial image is that of "self"; and, once created, man ever tends to enhance that image. This elevation of his own image necessarily implies the putting down of all others' images, however subtly; just as, collectively, the fostering of nationalism implies the depreciation of other nations and this eventually leads to conflict and war.

The image of a psychological self, the ego, was created on the basis of comparison, evaluation, against other egos. Thus, the roots of conflict are inherent in the ego — or self-image. Therefore, any efforts to deal with this violence without tackling the more fundamental problem of the ego are doomed from the start. Yet, this is what we see man doing: he has the wrong order of priorities. Rather than go to the bottom of this image-making process — in which lie the roots of his violence — he asks irrelevant, intellectual-type questions so that attention may be shifted away from where the real problem lies. For unconsciously man knows that so long as he engages in this frivolous play of thought-mind, the really painful process of fundamental self-facing — which eventually must lead to self-effacing — will be put off.

11 🦢

WORK WITHIN THE SYSTEM, OR WITHOUT?

Those who long to see a sane, rational and just society established, and wish to do something about it, are forever being exhorted by politicians of all colors and shades — and by their mouthpieces, the news media — to work exclusively "within the system." I would like to question this advice (if that's what it is).

In the first place, although many voices are yelling at us, almost hysterically, that the system works, does it in fact? Those who can observe what is happening in the world today, without this vision in any way being clouded by their vested interests in society, will be well aware that wars, poverty, racism, pollution, etc. are not problems that can be solved in isolation from one another. They are the inevitable symptoms of the rottenness of the system upon which this society's functioning is based; otherwise, these problems would have been solved long ago. We are using the word "rottenness" not in an emotional sense, but simply in its literal or dictionary meaning, since this best describes the actual situation. When something is rotten, it means that no cure, no relief, is possible without first cutting out the decaying part. So it is with society: because the very foundations are unsound, we have to start from scratch and try to set up an entirely different kind of community.

Personally, when I am being admonished to "work within our present system," my initial reaction is to say: "You may consider it *your* system, but it certainly is not *mine*. I may have inherited it willy-nilly from previous generations, but I did not invent it and feel in no way identified with, or responsible for, it. I see the possibility of working without the system; in fact, psychologically, I am already completely free from it, although at times I have to compromise and accommodate my actions to the system."

The new society which some of us envision (if it ever becomes actuality) will not be based upon this present system — and possibly not on a system of any kind. That society will be based on love; and is love to be confined within a system? Is compassion the result of some intellectual formula or an ideology? Do not say: that is altogether too idealistic; man will always compete, hate and kill. For we are saying something very practical and very urgent; that there are only two alternatives: a society ruled by greed, aggression and brute force, which will inevitably destroy itself; or a society based upon a true perception of reality, upon self-knowledge, which will result in a peaceful, orderly world. These are the only two choices open to man, there is nothing in between; the situation is as simple as that.

In few areas of thought do we see a greater chasm than here, between the advocates of the present system and those who reject that system because they can see clearly where it leads. Those who favor its preservation do not even question its foundations: they fight for the system because they are part of it. The politicians, the big-corporation boys, the law-enforcement officers — they would not even be what they are at present without their almighty system. What hypocrisy their advice then must be! They have done well by the system, they are grateful to it for they owe everything they have to that system. Does one really expect any impartiality from them?

On the other hand, those who view things in a different light are only saying: "See what a mess the world is in, which, in our view, is the direct result of your wretched system, which is based upon greed, self-interest and exploitation of the masses. No good can ever come out of it. Let us now try something else and give us the chance to do it, before it is too late."

12

NO MORE VIOLENT
CONFRONTATIONS

What is normally understood by a "policy of confrontation" is that ideology which seeks to achieve a vic-
tory over an oppressive, ruling clique by means of an
open clash, a violent meeting in the streets between the
mass of people and the guardians of the establishment.
The way I understand the situation, this is exactly the
policy which an oppressive government would dearly
love to see dissidents adopt, so that it can with relative
ease identify, and subsequently isolate or even eliminate
those who are considered to be a threat to its existence.
There are many historical precedents for this. A violent
revolution is therefore one of the most stupid things to
contemplate, not even taking into account that such tac-

tics totally lack any form of imagination or vision.

There is, however, a different kind of confrontation — the confrontation with what *is*, which is not only highly necessary but represents the only action that needs to be taken. From such a confrontation, a truly intelligent action will result — not one precipitated by fear, by one's aggression, by blindly following an ideology or by wishful thinking. Such an action will not be dictated merely by the pressure of circumstances, but will be based on a total understanding of the human situation from which these circumstances result. It will therefore be a complete action, rather than the usual fragmentary action which can have no more than a partial impact.

If one looks at things dualistically for one moment, for the sake of highlighting the issue, one might say that a lack of comprehension on the part of the masses is a major ally of the dominating group. "Power to the people" is an excellent slogan — as far as slogans go — but only if accompanied by real understanding of basic issues. Power without such understanding is absolutely useless, because it can be easily turned around by the oppressor who disposes of vastly superior means of physical violence; this might easily lead to destruction of the dissidents en masse. When, however, there is an intelligent appraisal of the many subtle ways in which a ruling class can exploit the masses to its own ends — by appealing to its lowest instincts, by intimidation, bribery, etc.— the oppressor can be given a dosage of his own medicine. This will cause confusion in his ranks and leave him without a counter. For, let us remember, no ruling power can keep its people down forever by the indiscriminate use of force and restrictions on individual freedom. It needs the cooperation of a certain number of "collaborators" and stool pigeons to succeed in its suppression; this means that the responsibility is thrown back at us, the people, to present a united front. If a sufficient number of people, out of their own self-knowledge, will have a clear vision of what has to be done, fearlessly, then a change in society must ensue. This change may initially not be so drastic or dramatic as that coming as the result of a violent confrontation, but through being based on what is, it will be all the sounder. After all, no structure can endure that is not built upon the right foundations.

The way to overcome an adversary of overwhelming strength is not to court a head-on collision, but to deal with it essentially in the spirit of the age-old wisdom of Taoism: to give way to it, but not to give in to it. It is only because the willow tree has the necessary suppleness and flexibility that it can withstand the onslaught of the fiercest snowstorms. Just so, must people with intelligence and patience absorb the forces of darkness.

13 🖎

HAS MAN A FUTURE?

Normally when this question is raised, we may have in mind the possibility of Doomsday — man wiping himself out either in a nuclear holocaust or through increasing pollution of his environment. With the present state of technology, that potentiality has now arrived for the first time in the history of the world. However, that we interpret the question in this particular way is because we always think of man collectively; but the "collective" has no actual existence except as an abstraction. There is only the individual; and no one ever asks himself whether individual man has a future, because he might make the uncomfortable discovery of the obvious: the unpalatable truth that man has no future at all. Every one of us is sentenced to die, and it is merely a question of time before the sentence will be carried out. Yet all our actions constantly belie that verity; we are ever building a platform for the ego that will withstand the ravages of time. It is as though by acting in this strange manner we can put off indefinitely the confrontation with what *is* (and what *is to be*). So, by ignoring our true nature, by not thinking of death too often — and when we do, preferably hedged about with myths about personal survival — we endeavor to escape serious mental discomfiture. And, in a sense, there is nothing wrong in ignoring something, if it were not for the fact that it is only the surface part of the mind which becomes forgetful; the deeper layers of the mind are only too well aware of man's finitude. Thus, there ever exists an obvious contradiction which engenders the fear that lies at the back of all our (escapist) activities.

Now it seems to me that if only man would realize the fact of his ephemeral nature on all levels of his being, and then live accordingly, he would not only banish that ever-present fear but create an altogether different world. By the middle course he is pursuing at present, of assigning a limited duration to the ego, he gets the worst of both worlds. On the one hand, it gives rise to a conflict situation in the psyche, and on the other, hand there is no difference between considering the ego as being of limited duration and its being of a permanent nature. Really, as soon as we assign the ego any existence at all in the present, we vouchsafe its future, for its very nature is continuity.

The world bears heavily the stamp of ego. Even the most non-egoist ideals ("for the sake of the nation, the party, the religion, etc....") are not free from the ego way of life. This, incidentally, is why we so readily identify with the collective and thereby contaminate the collective action. To understand why this must necessarily be so we must examine the nature of the ego. The ego has come about through the crystallization of certain attitudes in social interrelationships; it has only relative existence and is largely a kind of social mannerism. Imagine a man who has lived all his life on an uninhabited island and has never been exposed to human contact. His ego, his outlook and his thought-world must be of an entirely different character from that of the man living within society. If that much is clear, it may then be seen that ego formation is inherently an exploitative process; i.e., the ego has come about (and is nurtured at every moment) at the expense of other egos. We say: "I want to 'get ahead'," but what does "getting ahead" really mean? "Ahead of others," of course; thus, the whole process is comparative and my ego's flourishing necessarily implies the putting-down of some other ego(s). By asserting myself as "I am," I trample on other "be"ings. Logically extended, the same principle applies similarly to larger groupings, such as the family, the nation, and so on. The very establishment of such a collective entity is an act of aggression which leads to adversary relationships among these entities.

Thus, it is certainly no oversimplification to state that when man ceases to nurture ego, all strife in the world will come to an end; conversely, so long as man lives the ego way, strife and deterioration of society will be facts of life, no matter what he does. And so, paradoxically, only when man, individually, ceases to work at his future, will there be a future for man collectively.

14

THE GOLDEN RULE

I do not worship the so-called Golden Rule, the rule of doing unto others as you would have them do toward you. In fact, I don't think much of it at all. On a superficial level, it is so obvious that it tastes of a gimmick. But on a deeper level, it is not even true. For, in many cases the individual does not know where his best interests lie. What most of us want is to take the line of least resistance. But short-term gratification is often our worst medicine, leading to a perpetuation of our underlying malaise. Very few of us know ourselves sufficiently to understand what really ails us. So the opposite is more likely to be the case: What is good for us, hurts — especially on the spiritual level — and we would rather not have them do it toward us. To have all one's crutches taken away hurts. To be shown a mirror that clearly reflects our ugliness hurts; and it does not endear us to whomever it is that is responsible for such forceful confrontation, in the same way that people generally despise the messenger of bad news. Yet, the alternative is to strengthen all the forces of illusion and to ensure continuity to the realm of unreality. On a fundamental level, the Golden Rule is itself part of our painful dream-existence, and can never wake us up. The Golden Rule may lend encouragement to that most dangerous tribe, the Do-Gooders.

Now if someone were to insist on being given a rule of conduct, notwithstanding the fact that any such conduct would be totally incompatible with the spontaneous and unselfconscious action that takes place upon knowing oneself, what would one say? One would have to say to such a person: "Until you fully understand the nature of 'I Am,' do nothing intentionally that could hurt anyone." This is, as it were, a reversal of the Golden Rule, but one that is much more realistic and conducive to peace and harmony in the world.

15

"The High I.Q.'s Shall Inherit the Earth"

The news media have made much fuss about the existence of a sperm bank in California, in which the donors would all be Nobel Prize-winning scientists. It was pointed out, quite rightly, that such a measure smacked of elitism, not befitting a democracy, and was reminiscent of Nazi Germany with its emphasis on a pure race of "superior" beings and the elimination of "lesser" beings through sterilization and euthanasia. If man takes it upon himself to play God and decree who deserves to be born and who does not, then as a next step we must envisage the termination of those already born but not deserving of life in the eyes of Big Brother. We agree with all that; yet we wonder if the main point has not been lost altogether — namely, the standard which man has created based upon "intelligence" (as measured by the I.Q. tests and manifested by the cleverest of scientists) and also the whole idea of "superiority" and "inferiority."

The intelligence, as measured by the I.Q., which is essentially the capacity to exercise the discursive intellect, is not necessarily the main ingredient for the making of the Good Society. The Intelligence that is required is much more than the ability for linear thinking; it is the capacity to see things whole and to make oneself whole — so that one may live with Reality and not merely with an intellectual abstraction thereof. Now the curious thing is that this Intelligence cannot be manufactured by selective breeding, nor by training or by any effort whatsoever on man's part: it is not a function of time. To think that the Intelligence can be reached by such means is a direct outcome of the erroneous view that man is an island unto himself, separate as an individual from his fellow beings and the rest of creation — and that it is the brain that creates consciousness just like the liver produces bile. The truth of the matter is just the reverse: Only consciousness truly is, and every thing finds its existence by appearing in that consciousness as manifestation. The soma does not produce Intelligence, but Intelligence makes it possible for us to be aware of the soma.

Some may say: Isn't that a paradox?, because in order to reach out to the Intelligence which transcends my human limitations, I need that Intelligence in my search. To which, it seems to me, the answer must be: It is enough to use one's everyday common sense, one's so-called worldly intelligence, to see that the conventional explanations and solutions for man's predicament do not hold water, that there is no easy cure for the fundamental malaise of the human spirit, and above all, to see that it is the inner that is in turmoil and needs to be sorted out, before order can be produced in the outer, i.e., Society. Now such a sorting-out process needs, first of all, our undivided attention — as a detached observer — and the realization that any action other than that will only increase the chaos in the world. To be merely a do-gooder, whether on the inner or the outer level, is a retrograde step, a hindrance to the spiritual life. Basically then, our ordinary intelligence should enable us to see the various obstacles to a more enlightened way of functioning, and should be directed to them with a view to their removal. The very removal of the obstacles is enough — sufficient for the individual to participate richly in the life of the spirit, which draws upon the Infinite source of not only Intelligence but also Bliss. Man can reach Intelligence or the consciousness that transcends individuality by diving deep within himself at any time. It can be found in all its perfection and glory without delay. Nothing else is needed!

16

NEGATIVE IMAGINATION

In my negative imagination, I see a world in which
Political parties are nonexistent.
It is not necessary to confirm one's love with the words:
"I love you."
"Prejudice" does not exist: people are just people.
There is no difference between "work" and "play."
People do not "hire themselves out" to work, they just work
(or play, or work/play, or play/work —
whatever one wishes to call it).
There are no frontiers, no customs, no passports.
There is no difference between "I" and "Thou,"
and, therefore,
between "mine" and "thine."
There is time by the clock, but there is also the timeless —
and the latter pervades all consciousness, all activities.

There is no war, no need for the word "peace,"
in this connection,
for all people live in peace unthreatened.
Peace is not a political
concept, it has become a psychological
or religious term, and it *is* bliss.
There is no need for money,
because there is no "property" —
that is, private property.
There are no lawyers, no court disputes —
but there is justice.
There may be crime,
but there is no word for "criminals," with
its judgmental connotation.
Criminals are just unfortunate people,
patients in need of treatment.
There are no vested interests,
neither collective nor individual,
and because of that:
there is no fear of death — in fact, there is no longer a sharp
dividing line between living and dying.
There are no gurus, only disciples.
There are no religions, only religion.
There are no longer classes, strata in society — only people.
There is not the antithesis: poor and wealthy,
but a condition in which all have physical security.
There is no standard of living but there is quality of life.

There is sex (but it's no great deal) without guilt feelings.

There are no priests, no dogmas, no churches.
There is no spiritual "teaching,"
but an almost universal search,
a never-ending journey of discovery.
There are no monks, nuns, *sannyasins*, etc. —
but there is meditation
and there are a great many serious people.

The world thus sketched is different from Utopia,
which is the product of positive imagination,
that is, an extrapolation from our present Society, from our
present state of Ignorance.
Negative imagination is creative Emptiness;
all it does is take away
the conditioning, the rubbish,
from the mind, from the collective consciousness,
which has created the culture —
and look at what *is*, what *remains*.

People will say, well, all that is unrealistic, it is impossible, it is rubbish from my point of view — which is,
because they are using positive imagination, when it is
impossible, it is rubbish! You just can't get there from
here: either you are in this world or you are in that world
— there is no possibility of (gradual) transition.

Do not ask me: Is such a world at all possible, can it
be realized? All I will say is: You cannot get there from
where we are at present, under any circumstances. No
amount of reform, no revolution of any kind, can
change Society from *this* into *that* — for all such efforts

are based on positive imagination. Whether it is realizable —and that implies a mutation (in consciousness)— depends not on what one writer says. It depends on people, on human beings, and on the way they want to live. It depends on whether there is Love, in the real sense of the word — the Love by which all things become possible. But you may be quite right: such a Love may not be realistic, it may never be; people are essentially content with the world they have created. They are familiar with it, so that they can function in it, as it were, half-asleep; and maybe, from a negative imagination point of view, they are half-asleep, and they show as yet no sign of waking up.

17 〜

WHY DOES GOD ALLOW SUFFERING?

To me, the question is not "Why does God allow suffering?," but "Why does man tolerate suffering?" When the first question is put, we infer that there is suffering and there is man — the two are separate. But I maintain that man is Suffering; that is, man as he is constituted at present. It is his inherent nature, as much as wetness is the inherent nature of water.

It is not God that creates suffering and then metes it out on man, but man is the creator of his own suffering, the latter being inherent in the way he functions. So why blame God?

Man's actions are presently based on a very limited consciousness, only a dim awareness of cause-and-effect relationships. This deficient awareness is what Hindus call *Avidya*, or basic Ignorance. It is an Ignorance that is shared equally by the clever and the dumb, atheists and religionists, educated and non-educated.

Education, as formulated today in any academic context, does not address itself to *Avidya*. Thus, to overcome it, it is not knowledge of the fragmentary world that is missing and has to be acquired, but knowledge of the Ultimate. It is not a question of "being taught," but of "learning" — more particularly "self-learning." And by that expression we mean two things: learning by oneself, not as a group but individually, although in the framework of social relationship. And what one learns is the nature of oneself, and through that — and *only* through that — one comes upon the Ultimate. One learns the nature of one's identifications which together, although not always in unison, form the self that acts (but mostly re-acts) towards its environment. In actuality, it is not separate from its environment, but through its *Avidya* functions as though it is completely separate from the non-self.

And because all its reactions are ever self-defensive—that is, to defend itself from this environment — it is a vicious circle and can only deepen the illusion of separateness, fragmentation. Something is needed to break that vicious circle — a seeing with totally uninvolved eyes. The separation, the fragmentation, is *dukkha*, suffering — the pain of there being something amiss, of being non-whole. Only wholeness brings joy, bliss; and in such a world man, by his every action, demonstrates that he does not tolerate suffering. Only such seeing is capable of bringing about a transformation in man's inherent being. Just like water, when frozen, loses its inherent "wetness," so man, when fully awakened, loses his inherent fragmentation — he dissolves into the All. All "doing" based upon his mistaken identity stops. His suffering-prone nature has been transmuted.

18

THE PLEASURE TRAP

It seems that from the very beginning of time pleasure has had an overwhelming hold over all man's activities, as indeed it is symbolically represented in the creation story of the Christians. If one looks objectively at the human mind, one will see that it functions essentially in two modes. Its basic trend and manner of operating is simply to indulge in pleasure for its own sake — an undiluted, and originally innocent, hedonism. Because the mind does not know the joy which is not the result of pleasure, it has taken to the essentially hedonistic way of life to fill its own emptiness. And in the course of time, the mind has become blasé and dissipated. Having savored every kind of physical and psychological gratification to the point of satiation, the mind needs ever new and stronger titillations to keep its interest and drive away boredom and frustration. In this process, it has built a society whose particular psychological structure is increasingly based on the cultivation of pleasure.

As a result, pleasure has become a most complex thing. It has grown far beyond the response concomitant with the satisfaction of a simple physical need; all the mind's psychic energies now go towards securing and maintaining its pleasure inputs. This increasing dependency on gratification, mainly of a psychological kind, has necessarily brought in its wake a greater exposure to anxiety, frustration and fear. For, every activity of the mind towards its own gratification at once prepares the soil in which suffering is to take root. This is because pleasure and pain, in actual fact, are relative things — a pair of opposites that basically form a unity, like the two sides of a coin. However, since this interrelationship is none too conspicuous and pleasure usually evokes only a belated response as pain, man has always taken them for mutually independent absolutes — the one to be pursued and gathered, the other to be shunned. This attitude is very much like running hard to get away from one's shadow.

The second basic mode in which the human mind functions is to repress and sublimate pleasure; this mode is a reaction to, and is superimposed on, the way of indulgence. It grew out of the observation that unlimited individual indulgence had a disruptive influence on the life of the tribe. Thus, certain social restraints were instituted from which developed the concept of Morality. To enforce this morality, which was actually meant for the control of the masses and not strictly speaking for the conduct of the ruling class, it became necessary to invent revelationist religion, which put a stamp of absoluteness on moral edicts. All this began a long time ago when fear of the physical elements and of the Unknown induced a helpless and vulnerable *Homo sapiens* to invent an Almighty father figure to protect and fuss about him; and part of this "protection" consisted in the appropriate punishment whenever the moral precepts as laid down by the religious middlemen were flouted. But it is interesting to note that even today, when few people seriously believe in anything anymore, the Establishment — and by that word we mean the established organs of authority — continues its unholy alliance with organized religion and seeks to impose various arbitrary rules of moral conduct on the populace, thereby exploiting man's fears for the devious intents of a small clique.

Indulgence and repression operate side by side. There are relatively few individuals who are able to continually and unlimitedly indulge in pleasure for its own sake without running the risk of finding themselves locked up at an early stage. At the other end of the scale, there are a number of persons who, like the saints, seek to repress every form of pleasure. They live in a never-ending state of conflict, going as they are against the natural order of things, as it is a normal healthy response to react to pleasure stimuli which ceases only with the death of the organism. Yet, even these people are fundamentally pursuing pleasure, but in a more subtle and disguised form than the overt pleasure-seekers. They generally call it "virtue," but this kind of virtue is actually a most destructive thing.

Whether one is committed to hedonism or asceticism, the life that most of us know is a sequence of short-lived moments of pleasure, interlaced with periods of anguish — a sorry plight, for either way one is caught. Looking towards pleasure as the main goal of life means that, consciously or unconsciously, one draws up a balance sheet of pleasurable and painful events upon which one's happiness depends; and because the credit side of pleasure continually falls short of expectation, there is sorrow and life loses all meaning.

To this writer, the human condition as cursorily sketched above, is not an absolute. Because it is empirically found to be so, almost universally, one has unquestioningly accepted it as the only possibility: you know the old cliché about "human nature" supposedly cast of a particular, unalterable mold. Here, the exactly opposite view is put forward, that there is no such mold at all; paradoxically, the only mold that exists is the belief and acceptance that there is such a mold. In other words, our present way of functioning is not the result of an immutable, innate human make-up or destiny, but is brought about simply because we do not know, have never sought, another way.

I believe it was the Spanish thinker Ortega y Gasset who stated that man has the responsibility for "inventing his own life," which perhaps expresses rather well what we mean in this connection. That is, instead of inventing and seeking new forms of gratification, man should use his psychic energy and ingenuity to devise a new and saner way of living altogether, in which pleasure has its part to play but is no longer the predominant force. But even this still only states half the problem. If man is to come upon a new way of living, he must first totally re-make himself: fundamentally, there is no distinction between being and acting. Such a renewal can be brought about only by means of a penetrating under-standing of what he is at present. Man, all whose actions are instigated by the ultimate prospect of gratification, has to see very clearly through this whole question of pleasure, including its relationship to both action and time. If he can go that far in his meditation, it may lead him to absolute freedom from the pleasure trap. For the discovery may then be made that the mind can function in a third manner, which is neither indulgence nor repression, in which pleasure and pain are momentary experiences that no longer give rise to the demand for the more or the less.

19

JUST ONE LITTLE THING

There is just one little thing wrong with man,
Only one tiny, unsubstantial and intangible thing
But that can be quite a burden,
Depending on the nature of that "thing."

Man thinks there are a lot of matters
wrong with him.
That's why he studies many books,
learned journals, and searches out
numerous teachers
who go to great lengths to impress upon man
what ails him.

The more he searches, studies and listens to others
and never takes the trouble to look within,
to explore his innermost mental being,
the more confused man gets.
And that one little thing ever eludes him.

It's a disease he is the carrier of,
and knows nothing about.

He does not and cannot relate
the symptoms to the cause
and so ever passes its malevolent
germ on to others, equally unaware.
The name of this disease is EGO.

Ego is given to us by others,
We do not and cannot produce it
by ourselves.
Without others, no ego.
Society, paradoxically, a multiplicity itself
imposes on each his role, his function,
and so manufactures a mold,
in the shape of "individuality," so-called.

Society also brings us "good" and "bad,"
and the discrimination thereof,
and thus the entire state
of duality in which we unconsciously function.

Without society, things just are —
and that is "good" — a state of pristine purity,
which one might also spell "God," "Emptiness,"
but the word does not matter:
A state of Happiness, Peace, Bliss.
Who cares about verbal descriptions
that are mere symbols, ever insufficient

to reach that which is utterly beyond words and thought,
When Being, not Becoming, is our condition
and Past, Present, and Future have merged, disappeared
as separate entities, never to hassle us again
with feverish imaginations, fears, doubts
when there is only That, Suchness, Eternity.

PART TWO

20

MORALITY AND SPIRITUALITY

The self-realized man, who has firmly established himself in the identity of the Self, which is the self of all and everything, is not subject to Morality: he verily is Morality. Living in a state of love, he is the essence of goodness, and this Goodness transcends that which the mind would understand as "right" and "wrong."

Morality applies only to those who have not yet found themselves, who are still functioning as mere fragments, who do not know true Wholeness. For them, "rightness" is all those actions that bring them closer to such a state of Wholeness (or holiness) and "wrongness" all those actions that fortify them in their state of isolation. In other words, for them the greatest good is to get rid of the ego, which is what keeps them from realizing their true essence. This is the only "morality" based on reality — all other schemes of morality are man-made and, therefore, products of the collective consciousness.

The mind is ever anxious to ask questions about

morality because, knowing its own dangerous tendencies, it paradoxically seeks protection from itself. Because
the mind is totally ignorant about itself and hardly has a
desire to learn, it rarely asks questions about liberation.
It sets greater store by morality than liberation, yet the
latter would obviate its concern with the former.

The *Upanishads* confirm the views expressed above.
For example, the *Mundaka Upanishad* states: "When the
seer beholds the . . . Supreme Being, then, transcending
both good and evil, and freed from impurities, he unites
himself with him." And also: "Thus Brahman is all in all.
He is action, knowledge, *goodness supreme.* To know him,
hidden in the lotus of the heart, is to untie the knot of
ignorance." About the false morality of good works or
"do-gooding," this Upanishad is equally outspoken:
"Considering religion to be observance of rituals and
performance of acts of charity, the deluded remain ignorant of the highest good. Having enjoyed in heaven the
reward of their good works, they enter again into the
world of mortals." And in the *Brihadaranyaka
Upanishad* one reads, much in the same vein: "Nay, even
if a man ignorant of the kingdom of the Self should do
virtuous deeds on earth, he would not arrive through
them at everlasting life: for the effects of his deeds would
finally be exhausted. Wherefore let him know the kingdom of the Self, and that alone. The virtue of him who
meditates on the kingdom of the Self is never exhausted:
for the Self is the source from which all virtue springs."
(Italics are mine, RP)

Finally, the *Chandogya Upanishad* sums it up tersely,

as follows: "Through insight we understand all branches of learning, and we understand what is right and what is wrong, what is true and what is false, what is good and what is bad . . . ."

21 ❧

SOME OBSERVATIONS ON UPANISHADS AND EARLY GREEK THOUGHT

One interesting aspect of the Upanishads is that they apparently had the edge on the early Greek thinkers in a very fundamental way. Among the latter we find preoccupation with cosmological inquiries into the nature of the physical world which precedes inquiries into the manner by which that knowledge was acquired. In a sense, therefore, they had the cart before the horse so long as the origin and therefore the validity of that knowledge remained unclear. Only gradually did problems of knowledge and the knower come into prominence, and so only gradually did a deliberate trend toward reflection on the inner, as distinguished from the outer, become evident.

On the other hand, the Upanishads were right there, from the very beginning, dealing with such questions as

"Who is the knower?" and concluding that the knower is the known ("Thou art That").

A few Greek thinkers seem to have taken some tentative steps in this direction and made a modest contribution towards a theory of knowledge. For example, Empedocles stated that like can only be known by like. He believed that since man has knowledge of the elements composing the Universe, he himself must be made up of those same elements. Thus, man knows water because particles of water pass to the eye and are there contacted by identical particles in the eye. "This contact of water with water enables man to know water." His thesis can therefore be viewed as a theory of self-identification. We find the Universe back within ourselves and only for that can we know the world outside. As within, so without!

Empedocles also stated that nothing can arise from nothing, nor can anything disappear into nothing. There is only a continual rearrangement of permanent entities in a closed system. We see here some resemblance to the modern physicists' law of the conservation of mass-energy. Probably, from this conviction that nothing ever disappears stemmed Empedocles' belief in reincarnation.

Taken literally, Empedocles' main proposition, that like can be known by like, is plainly untenable. In the conventional sense of knowing as re-cognition, definition, and measurement, like can be known only by unlike, by something more evolved, more refined, or more complex. In this respect, an analogy from science may be helpful to get the point. A light microscope cannot detect or "see" particles of a certain small size if they are of the same order of magnitude as light's wavelength. But an electron microscope, employing a much smaller wavelength, can easily do so, although its own image definition is similarly limited.

Of course, in a deeper sense, in which to know something means to be that, Empedocles' proposition begins to make sense, and as such it may be viewed as symbolic, foreshadowing the insight of non-duality in which the knower is the known.

After Empedocles, we will consider Anaximander, who was perhaps the first philosopher in the West to teach that the Real was the One, the "Apeiron," as he called it (literally, that which has no boundary), the Infinite, the Eternal, out of which everything arises, and into which everything returns. In a similar vein, Plotinus asserted that "to know" the One — which to him lay beyond the subject-object duality and, therefore, beyond knowledge in the accepted sense — one must become one with it, which takes place in a condition of "ecstasy" (literally, being beside oneself). And for this to be possible, he advised his students: "Strip yourself of everything," by which he presumably meant: "Empty the mind totally."

Then there was Parmenides, who relegated "becoming" to the realm of opinion and regarded "being" as the only actuality. Maybe, he intuitively understood the unreality of space-time. His disciple Zeno was the father of the method of *reductio ad absurdum*, which I personally have always found extremely helpful in its function as a supreme thought-experiment in throwing light on all types of problem situations. Derivative of this principle is the construction of a "worst-case scenario," which can be a useful test of one's capacity for "letting go," so difficult yet so necessary in the spiritual life.

Another Greek thinker, Heraclitus, came very close to the Hindu/Buddhist concept of existence as birthless and deathless. He believed the world to be uncreated; that is, it needed not be created simply because it has always existed. All events take place according to a "Logos" (governing principle, Intelligence) and unity of opposites; all things are in a flux, like a river. Likewise, Plotinus stated there had never been a non-existent Universe. Both Plato and Plotinus viewed time as a mere empirical reality.

Finally, the Greek philosopher who may well have come closest to the ultimate Upanishadic insight and who, at least partly, espoused a realistic "theory of knowledge" was Protagoras, who stated that "man is the measure of all things." The words apparently contain great wisdom, but I do not know to what extent he realized their implications. They are the forerunner of the realization that man's thought is essentially, what is named in current terms, "closed-circuit thinking" and is thereby strictly limited. Thus, we define "things" and even ideas ever in terms of what we already know, what we are familiar with. Unbeknownst to us, they are really self-referential statements (and as such, are likely to lead to paradox). This applies in relation to our physical as well as psychological world. How could it be otherwise? Thus, the unknown is always translated in terms of the known. With any problem, the answer is contained in the question! Thus, all our knowledge consists of an endless series of reference systems, always deferring the solution as to what *is*; that is, describing, explaining, yet leaving the necessity for further clarification in the same manner, and so never "arriving," never knowing in the deepest sense. We are full of explanations, but this is actually merely buck-passing through a gigantic con system of semantics (or mathematics, as in science). We always seem to forget that the word (or the mathematical symbol) is not the thing! This activity is paralleled in our spiritual search: ever *seeking*, but never *finding*; ever *talking about*, but never *dealing with* issues. Because the solution, which is supposed to be the "new," is part of the problem, which is, of course, the "old," every solution represents a fresh problem that in turn needs solution, and so on ad infinitum; thus, we are ever going around in circles. This is the essential nature of closed-circuit reasoning, in which the new cannot enter.

Normally, we are not aware of this process until we begin to dig really deep, on a fundamental level. Then one arrives inevitably at a dead end or is left dangling with a paradox, which forces one to revise his initial assumptions and to take an entirely different approach that will have nothing to do with closed-circuit reasoning. But for this, man must go beyond the measure of his mind, beyond his innate *Maya*, as is so clearly indicated in the Upanishads.

To return to Protagoras, he further held the relativist

position that things are for me as they appear to me, and for another as they appear to him. Sensation is actual, and free from error; that is, it gives correct knowledge. Protagoras was not asserting a doctrine of "subjectivism"; he is not suggesting that the world as perceived by the senses is a mental state of the percipient. But he indicates that we are not entitled to assume a common real world apprehensible by any number of percipients — each percipient lives in a private world of his own.

Thus, one important aspect of Protagoras' famous statement is that perception is always an individualized affair. That is, each lives in a private world, as recorded by the mind-senses, and to speak of a "common experience" or a common basis of knowledge is meaningless. In my book *Crisis in Consciousness* (p. 106), I have discussed this subject and shown how language actually hides from us individual differences in perception. "Language only makes us refer to the same things, but that is all it does . . . we are never aware of this because it is impossible to communicate these experiences to others except in terms of language . . . and there the vicious circle closes again."[1]

Knowledge must be apprehended as a relationship. All knowledge is therefore relative to the observer. Then, the next step is to realize that there is no difference between the "thing in itself" and the thing as it appears to us — or as we "know" it. Alternatively, one might say there exists no such thing as a "thing in itself," for the latter term becomes meaningful only in relation to an observer! This last statement is, however, not the same as

[1] *Crisis in Consciousness*, Sun Publishing Company, Santa Fe, New Mexico, 1988.

saying that nothing exists — a total vacuum, as it were— without the presence of an observer, as some modern philosophers nevertheless seem to do. The point here is that "thingness" comes into being automatically with the presence of an observer.

In sum, when surveying the field of the most enlightened Greek thinkers of the classical period, one gets the feeling that however close some of them came to the truth of the Upanishads, which is the truth about the Self, essentially they were still held by logic, by a dependence on the existence of "things," and had not come to terms with the notion of "thingness." We note a reliance on "ideas," on knowledge of the external world, as being separate from the inner world; and it is probably from this source that we have inherited our exaggerated reverence for science as an alleged means of discovering ultimate reality and a way station on the spiritual path.

22

BIRTHLESS AND DEATHLESS

We have assumed, or accepted from hearsay, that we are born and die, yet we have no experiential evidence thereof. At no time did we experience a beginning of our beingness, and at no time shall we experience an ending of our beingness. Such an alleged beginning and ending is actually only postulated by others and imposed on us as certain knowledge. What we take to be our birth is only an appearance — the appearance of a body to others — and what we take to be our death is only the destruction of that body to others. The "me" is never aware of either phenomenon. The birth in actuality is an identification of consciousness with that body — leading to the beginning of a pseudo-entity — and dying and the point of death cannot be an actual experience either. The consciousness that has identified itself with the body will function only so long as the psychosomatic process is proceeding; when it ends because the vital function has stopped, there is no consciousness to undergo and record this experience. But what we are is not merely this consciousness that is time-bound, being limited to the duration of the body and rooted in some "personality," in memory. The essence of what we are lies beyond experience, or non-experience for that matter: consciousness never knows a state of nonexistence, neither of "me" nor "world," the concept of nonexistence always being projected from "existence" and so utterly unreal. Thus, there is ever "I am" only, a state which is birthless and deathless.

23 ~~

WHO AM I?—
THE IMPOSSIBLE QUESTION

To my mind, the most pertinent question that man can ask himself is "Who am I?" Any other question, such as "What am I here for?" or "What is the significance of my life?" is strictly secondary and becomes redundant to the man who pursues the first question with alacrity and energy. All those other questions are necessarily secondary, because explicitly or implicitly they center around an "I." Now how can they be meaningful in a fundamental sense so long as one has not dealt in an adequate way with the nature of that "I"?

From the earliest recorded spiritual discourses to modern days, the question "Who am I?" has served as the master key to the understanding of man and his universe. The Upanishads, a few thousand years ago, discuss it, and so — in one way or another — do all enlightened sages throughout history, including in more recent times Ramana Maharshi, J. Krishnamurti and Nisargadatta.

In the East, many people believe that from time immemorial, ever since man became a self-conscious creature, he has inquired into his identity, and that as a result the universal wisdom of the Upanishads has always been with him. During earlier cycles of civilization, records of which have long been lost, this perennial wisdom was passed on from generation to generation through either oral transmission or scriptures. Thus, even in the darkest periods of man's history, individuals lived who were capable of passing on the torch of truth so that the light of the world would not go out completely. Intuitively, one feels all this to be true, because where it concerns the realization of timeless and universal insights, man is not affected by such incidentals as time and place.

Now the question "Who am I?" has tremendous importance and potency for two reasons. First of all, where else could man start his inquiry if not from where he finds himself in the moment? It requires no travel to faraway places and his field of observation and study is always right in front of him, closer than anything else, and totally accessible. Because people always look for the truth afar, it is most often overlooked that the treasure lies at their very doorstep. Second, nothing — absolutely no other issue — can be clearly understood until one first comes to grips with his identity. It is quite clear why this must be so. Man sees the world through his mind's eye. Thus, the mind, his inherent being, is what determines his observation of the Universe. The power of the collective consciousness is such that after early infancy there is not a single mind left untouched by conditioning. It is this conditioning background that intervenes in every observation — filtering and coloring all experience. Nisargadatta stated in this connection: "Everybody sees the world through the idea he has of himself . . . If you imagine yourself as separate from the world, the world will appear as separate from you and you will experience desire and fear." And Protagoras' "Man is the measure of all things" points in the same direction.

It must be emphasized that the importance for man lies in putting the question, in starting the inquiry — not in coming up with an answer. What, anyway, could be the answer? Any answer would necessarily be in the form of some verbal formula, a set of images or concepts, and let us remember: the word is not the thing, a symbol is different in itself from what it symbolizes, a concept is the very antithesis of what *is*. The word, the symbol, the concept, stand in the same relationship to their underlying realities as a shadow to the object which has cast it: they lack entirely in substance. And, what is worse, any such explanatory terms are themselves based on arbitrary assumptions about the self and the world. Such assumptions are built into the very words and symbols through lack of understanding and noninvestigation; and so the whole thing becomes a subtle form of begging the question, a cyclical argument beyond which the discursive intellect can never go. Under those circumstances, defining the nature of one's self would be like trying to grasp the air inside one's fist. The self is a vastness too immense, too subtle, too deep, too fluid, to be pinned down in any manner whatsoever.

In the conventional sense, "Who am I?" is therefore an impossible question, because *it simply has no answer*. Now this fact, however, is no justification for not asking the question. In this particular case, the value of the question lies in the asking, in the inquiry, not in the answering. Not answering, not needing to answer it, means that one can pursue the inquiry, go very deep, without being sidetracked by the irrelevancies of words and symbols. Thus, one stays with the question, lets the question work its own magic. And in doing that, something unprecedented takes place. There is an immediate liberation from the misleading terms of reference which form the backbone of our conditioning. There is an opening up into a new dimension, in which there is complete understanding of oneself, of man's true identity, a wordless knowing of what one is, and at the same time—not one split second afterwards — an understanding of the "world" around oneself and a deep realization that one is that world.

24

CLEARING THE SEMANTIC FOG AROUND OUR SELF

The word is not the thing, yet we always seem to demand words and explanations, especially in the spiritual realm where they are least applicable. We are inclined to forget that words are mere codes referring to recurring experiences and observations. The codes are meaningful to each of us only because the underlying experience or observation is of the recurring type, and therefore of the known. Use of the word implies re-cognition, a repeat of the old; but with the totally new, which is the unknown, words are at a loss to convey the experience. Since each of us lives in a private world of his own, the words and concepts are useful only for our own orientation and to cue another person in to his chain of repeated, and therefore familiar, experiences (this cuing is what we call "communication"). But they are powerless to convey the exact underlying experience from one to another, just as it is not possible to convey what color is to a blind person or music to a deaf one.

In this connection, it is interesting that the words "experience" and "experiment" have the same etymological root. Thus, each of us is having his own experiences, or doing his own unique "experiments" on the environment. For example, when talking about the sweetness of sugar, each of us is merely reminded of his own experience of sweetness ("experiment" with sugar). But how to convey my own experience of "sweetness" to a person born without sense of taste? And, how exactly do I convey my own experience of "sweetness" to you, so that you may compare my experience with your experience of "sweetness"? On a deeper level, I feel that because of the experiential impossibility of the questions, even as thought experiments, the questions are invalid and the underlying assumptions incorrect.[1] Because of the overall relativity of our entire world experience, such questions will always lead to paradox and meaninglessness. I feel this is a similar situation to another question I have asked myself: Is it possible in any scientific measurement to obtain an absolutely exact (i.e., final) value from one's instruments? Such a result could be obtained only if the observer and the thing observed were two distinct realities. However, the latter assumption is true only as an

---

1 It is somewhat analogous to the situation in basic scientific exploration, where an experiment that cannot be done for any reason, not even as a thought experiment, means that the whole framework of scientific reasoning within which it is conceived, is invalid. For example, if the whole world in which we live were to be increased or reduced in size a thousandfold overnight, no experiment would be able to measure it, for our yardsticks would be equally affected. This upsets the age-old assumption of absolute space.

Similarly, the famous Michelson-Morley experiment that failed to measure the so-called ether wind, led to the bringing down of not only the theory of the ether but also the entire Newtonian world view.

approximation, for ultimately the observer and the observed are intimately related; in fact, they are "not-two," but part of one continuum. Expressed differently, one may say that the experience and the experienced ever stand in a unique relationship and that experience per se, as an absolute, is nonexistent — a mental abstraction. Thus, the idea of conveying experience from one person to another is a fallacy, and any words to that effect are merely begging the question. And, analogously, to obtain the absolutely correct scientific measurement must ever elude the experimenter, for the latter is not separate from the experiment and the thing to be measured.

All that has been stated thus far may appear to be irrelevant but is actually a necessary prelude to the question of the Self, which is the unknown. We have already seen that to approach the Self we must follow the negative way, on account of its ineffable character. That is to say, all the images, the many concepts we hold of the Self must be stripped away for the real Self to be uncovered. For in the aggregate, they describe merely the apparent or false self, that which we take ourselves to be by believing in the creations of our imagination. It follows then that the Self is never to be defined in terms of words, concepts or images — for, by definition, these can only appertain to the non-Self. It has also been said — and this comes to the very same thing — that all that we can ever know is that which is not our Self. In investigating oneself, this is something that must be constantly borne in mind.

So, whenever anyone asks one to give a definition of

the Self, he is faced with an impossible question: it is the one thing that absolutely defies definition, or even description. All that one can do is hint at the Self, and then only in negative terms: Not this, not that . . . In other words, the Self cannot be "known," it must forever remain the Unknown. Thus, when anyone uses the term "Self-knowing," he is actually referring to "not-Self knowing." But why should one want to know the Self, in terms of words, which, after all, are symbols and concepts—when one *is* that very Self? Is it not sufficient to eat one's dinner without wanting to consume the menu as well?

Thus, what is needed is to realize that one is the Self, to understand this so thoroughly that one no longer acts as though being a stranger to oneself — that is, confused, in eternal conflict, a mere bundle of fragmented role-playing entities. This understanding is what is called "Self-Realization" — and unlike mere "knowing," brings into being a qualitatively different state of being, a veritable transformation in consciousness, which transcends knowledge itself and thus obviates the intellectual approach to the truth about oneself. It must be stated here that statements by those who have realized themselves, in the form of "hints" about the Self, show a remarkable "sameness," even coming from individuals with totally different backgrounds. Although constituting no absolute proof, this is a powerful argument for the veracity of their vision. It shows that mere incidentals of birth and upbringing play no part in the realization of that which is truly universal and untainted by the limitations of space and time.

Since the Self is the great Unknown, and to live with that does not give us any certainty or security, most of us have substituted "certain" knowledge of our own making. Apparently, the universal principle in physics that states that nature abhors, and therefore ever tends to fill, a vacuum, applies also in the psychological sphere. Rather than living in and by the Self — which is just living, without ideation about the tomorrow, albeit living supremely — we have opted to depend upon this certain knowledge, which is always of the past and gives us a (false) sense of security. And, of course, that knowledge could only be of the know-able, which, as we have seen, is the non-Self. In other words, we have allowed ourselves to fall into the trap of a lifelong fixation on an entity which we ourselves have created from thought and memory. Although this entity has absolutely nothing to do with the Self — our real nature — we have, paradoxically, chosen to call it "self." Once this "self" has been established and taken hold of our consciousness, even though it is no more than a dream entity or a figment of our imagination, our whole world revolves around it; in tyrannical fashion, it dictates all our thoughts and actions.

That this entity is not our real Self must be clearly seen through perceiving its unreality. The apparent self has come about as the cumulative product of many yesterdays, a set of selective images and concepts without any real substance, bound together and given apparent substance by memory through a kind of mental optical illusion. It is somewhat analogous to the spokes of a fast-turning wheel appearing as one solid surface. After all, how can what has been be real, when we mean by "real" that which is (now)? Is yesterday's sunset real today? The fact that the images, etc. are memories, past experiences, signifies by definition that they are not actual, real in the present. Yesterday's sunset is as unreal today as tomorrow's sunset. The *Katha Upanishad* states quite clearly: "There are two selves, the *apparent* self and the *real* Self." Unfortunately, subsequent interpretation of this very simple and unambiguous statement has corrupted it into postulation of "a higher and a lower self." In view of our foregoing discussion, it must be immediately clear that such a statement, with the attributes of "higher" and "lower," could not possibly apply to the non-definable, the Self, but only to the non-Self. Since we are not interested in basing our life upon the unreal, there is obviously no point in further pursuing this line of investigation. It would be tantamount to seeking to wake up from our dreams of unreality through an analysis and interpretation of these very same dreams.

What man's hidden motives are in accepting and clinging to the erroneous concept of the higher and the lower self is another story. It allows him to set up an illusory scenario in which there is an endless battle between the higher and the lower part of him — or, what he calls the forces of good and evil — in which gradually the higher self takes the upper hand. Thus, man has a marvelous ploy to evade the real issues of the here-and-now and procrastinate *ad infinitum* with the inner work of a radical transformation in consciousness. But, since it is ever the Now that deter-

mines the future, any reliance on gradualism will only perpetuate the status quo of man's condition.

J. Krishnamurti has frequently exposed the thesis of
the higher and lower self as a total aberration in the spiritual quest. However, from talking with people who pro-
fess to be serious students of Krishnamurti, I have noted
that the area still abounds with misunderstandings. For
example, the denial of the division of our being into a
higher and a lower part is taken by some as the complete
denial of Self. They are misinterpreting his teaching and
putting words in his mouth that he never uttered.
Because on occasion he has said that the "individual"
does not exist, they take this to mean that there is no
Self. But the absurdity of their thesis must be obvious at
once, for if the Self does not exist, who is it that is asserting this? The very denial of myself necessarily implies an
affirmation, even only on the level of logic. And
although Krishnamurti may not use the word Self as
such, he has referred to it by various other terms, such as
the Beloved, the Ground, the Otherness, the Sacred, *et
al.* Lest it be thought he is thereby referring to realities
other than Self, he has specifically stated the opposite
(e.g., "The Beloved and me are One.") and uses every
opportunity to emphasize what he calls the "indivisibili-
ty" of Reality. The latter term is, of course, synonymous
with the more familiar "non-duality," or *Advaita,* as it is
named in the Orient.

Finally, there are those who talk about the so-called
"little self" and "large self." Since they have read these
terms in Oriental philosophical writings, they take them

at face value, not realizing that these are code words for the apparent self and the real Self. In other words, the little self is not our Self at all, but is the unreal entity referred to before as the synthetic "me." And the large self, as opposed to the little self, is really a misnomer because the real Self, as we have seen, cannot be qualified in any way whatsoever. Moreover, the Self is not one term of a pair of opposites but lies beyond all opposites and beyond all concepts.

After wading through all these confounding expressions, originating partly from lack of insight and partly from semantic limitations, what have we got left? Obviously, what remains only is the Self, which is the Absolute underlying all relative existence, comprising everything yet itself being beyond all and everything. Besides our Self nothing exists, and of the whole of Existence there is nothing that is not the Self. As it is hinted at in the *Katha Upanishad*, "Soundless, formless, intangible, undying, tasteless, odorless, without beginning, without end, eternal, immutable, beyond nature, is the Self. Knowing him as such, one is freed from death."

25 ❧

FROM THOUGHT TO INSIGHT: AN UNBRIDGEABLE GAP

At the time of writing this part of the book (summer, 1984), by a strange coincidence a rather unusual (i.e., for a newspaper) but highly relevant public interchange of ideas took place in the Letters columns of the Book Review section of the *Los Angeles Times*. It started with a review in the same paper (August 5) by the Times Science Writer, Lee Dembart, of *Understanding Relativity: Origin and Impact of a Scientific Revolution* by Stanley Goldberg (Birkhauser, Boston, 1984).

Dembart writes that the author has not succeeded in proving his central thesis that the "fate of ideas like the theory of relativity is as much a function of culture as is the fate of any other product of the human intellect." He further states: "Goldberg's assertion that 'any set of experimental evidences can be explained from any theoretical point of view one wants to adopt' makes the laws of nature sound like inventions of man's mind. There is a real world out there. Scientists are subject to all the human foibles but over the centuries, science has progressed to greater understanding of nature's secrets, which have an existence of their own. Goldberg is . . . wrong to insist that social factors are more important in scientific knowledge than truth is."

Interestingly, in 1960, the correspondence columns of *The New Scientist* (January 28, p. 225) revealed a very similar controversy, which I fully reported and discussed in my book *The Great Awakening* (pp. 151-154).[1] That correspondence started with a letter writer asking readers of the journal whether science should be considered the pursuit of truth, or whether it was perhaps something entirely different. And is there such a thing as an absolutely correct scientific measurement, or is this a mere concept in the mind? What about the values of the so-called physical constants in nature (e.g., Planck's Constant)? Are they to be considered absolute and therefore have a definite, exact value, or are they relative and therefore approximate?

One person replied very aptly and lucidly as follows:

> To speak of a scientist as a seeker of truth is a colloquialism which, if interpreted too literally, may mislead us as to the correct nature of the physical world. The scientist, in attempting to explain a natural phenomenon, does not look for some underlying true phenomenon but tries to

1 The Great Awakening, Theosophical Publishing House, Wheaton, Illinois, 1983.

invent a hypothesis or model whose behaviour will be as close as possible to that of the observed natural phenomenon. As his techniques of observation improve and he realizes that the natural phenomenon is more complex than he originally thought, he has to discard his first hypothesis and replace it with another, more sophisticated one, which may be said to be "truer" than the first, since it resembles the observed facts more closely.

I further commented: ". . . the scientist is simply seeking a new hypothesis which fits the observed phenomena better than did a previous one; but this is still within the sphere of 'models' of the universe, of reality — and that is all he is concerned with. Therefore, he is *not* seeking Truth, for if he were he would at once give up the effort to 'reconstruct' reality by means of models and mathematical equations which at best can have the same relation to Reality as a photographic image has to its original (it lacks a full dimension!). In other words, the scientist lives in a world of abstractions; he is only concerned with 'making things work' by systematized common sense." Therefore, Dembart is wrong to mention scientific knowledge and truth in the same breath. He is also wrong to maintain that nature's secrets can have an existence of their own, independent of the human observer. As modern physics is discovering more and more and as we have never tired of pointing out in this and other writings: The observer and the observed are ever in close relationship, and on the most fundamental level *the observer is the observed.* This applies on both the material level and the psychological level. Thus, although I would not like to characterize the laws of nature as "inventions of man's mind," they are necessarily cast in the same mold as man's sensory and mental make-up. These laws simply cannot be divorced from the essential mode of functioning of human beings.

Although ultimately all issues are interrelated, we need not dwell upon the strictly scientific aspects, since this is not a book on the philosophy of science. What is more of concern to us is the underlying doubt about the reality of the physical world in view of its psychological implications. That is why the following letters were thought to be of some interest to readers of this book.

Relative Reality

Regarding Lee Dembart's review of Stanley Goldberg's "Understanding Relativity" (Book Review, Aug. 5), I am writing to deplore the wrong-headed dogmatism with which the reviewer summarily rejects the book's theses.

One does not have to be a solipsist or believe that the world is a dream to realize that the "real world" is nothing but an assumption, corresponding to a practical attitude, that is not only wholly unverifiable but probably devoid of meaning. As for the laws of nature being inventions of man's mind, this is obviously the case, in the strict sense. The question is how and why man came to invent them.

Lucas Kamp
Pasadena

Dare He Tell Holyfield?

So Lucas Kamp (Letters, Aug. 12) has realized—though not dogmatically — that the "real world" is nothing but an assumption, corresponding to a practical attitude, that is not only wholly unverifiable but probably devoid of meaning.

Maybe he ought to try to convince a battered wife of that, or a molested child, or a Vietnam vet in a wheelchair. They'd probably find it hard to understand how anyone could say something so devoid of meaning.

Of course, if he decides to mention this profound insight to Olympic boxer Evander Holyfield, I'd suggest that he keep his unverifiable nose well out of reach of Holyfield's practical attitude. Otherwise, Kamp's unverifiable assumptions may not last any longer than his unverifiable consciousness.

Philip Blackmarr
Pasadena

In response to the above interchange of ideas, I sent

off the following letter to the *Los Angeles Times* Book Review, which never got published. The editor, Mr. Art Seidenbaum, wrote me a note of apology, explaining that the paper does not run rebuttals to rebuttals for fear of overtaxing readers' memories.

"Such Stuff as Dreams are Made on . . ."

Philip Blackmarr's introduction of the red herring of the battered wife, etc. (Letters, Aug. 26) into the controversy over the reality of the world simply will not do in disposing of the issue. What Mr. Blackmarr, in effect, is saying is that life is painful, full of anguish; therefore, it must be real. But so is a nightmare. Is it therefore real, viewed from the waking state? Amputees often suffer pain in a limb recently amputated (the so-called "ghost limb"). The lesson: Pain in itself does not prove reality. And, more generally, things are not what they appear to be; our sensory impressions are apt to deceive us. On a fundamental level, there is an even more serious objection to his thesis, overriding all other considerations: Contending or implying that the world is real is no less devoid of meaning than the opposite. What, after all, are one's yardsticks of reality? There is none; for any such "standard" would itself be part of the world, part of that which is to be proved — a subtle form of begging the question.

Lucas Kamp's statement (Letters, 12 Aug.) that

the world is of the nature of a dream, an assumption, has a great depth of meaningfullness to it if used as the starting point for further inquiry. I think what he is hinting at is the possibility of awakening into a different state of consciousness in which our present "realities" are seen to be like things perceived in a dream. An approach toward this vision may be the following. What we experience as the world "out there" is merely a stream of sensory impressions, processed by the brain as perceptions, and ending up as thoughts arising in the mind. The "out there" is a thought among thoughts, but it sets the tone for our entire dualistic mode of functioning. An analogous thing happens in our dreams, and we are similarly hoodwinked into believing in the reality of the dream "theater" until the dream ends or we "wake up." Thus, the onus is on those who hold to the objective reality of the world to prove it so; i.e., that these sensory impressions are indeed caused by objects existing on the outside rather than within consciousness.

Unlike the useless theological conundrums of the past (e.g., how many angels can balance on the head of a pin), such an insight can have immense value for living in this real/unreal world in a sane manner.

Robert Powell
La Jolla

Final Note:

The outcome of the inquiry that the world is nothing but a dream can in itself — that is, as new knowledge or a "conclusion"— do nothing to help us in coping with our everyday life. However, as an insight that spills over into our understanding of what one is as an individual, and especially that one is not in the world but the world is within oneself, it can open the door to an entirely new way of functioning. Is this not what meditation is all about? In the following chapters of this book, we shall go into the matter more deeply.

26 ～

THE RAZOR-EDGED PATH

What are the problems confronting the novice on the spiritual path? First of all, there must be some inner need for anyone to embark on such a journey. The vast majority of people in the world do not know what it is all about, and so have absolutely no interest in the subject. And why should they? Apart from an occasional vague feeling of emptiness, which is soon filled by outer activities of various kinds, they have — consciously or subconsciously — resigned themselves to their fates. Thus, "spiritual" remains a mere word without any existentialist significance. These people have no inkling that a totally different way of functioning is not only possible but also is actually man's intended "natural state." They do not understand that man has lost this state through his own doing, his perverted way of looking at the world and himself. In their youth, they may have been aware of the chaotic and harsh conditions of the outer world, but they soon resigned themselves to these circumstances and adjusted their thinking rather than staying faithful to their original sensitivities. This is what the conforming pressures of their peers and elders have done to them, when they took the norm for the natural state. They have taken the outer state, the society, as the model into which their own individual selves had to fit, thereby perpetuating the human predicament in which a confused mind ever spreads more confusion in the world at large.

Then, there are others who have a mere semantic acquaintanceship with the term "spiritual." For example, when coming across a man like J. Krishnamurti or Nisargadatta, they assume that the teaching of these men concerns some abstract philosophy that one pursues for excitement, to be different, or to add sophistication to one's life. In a sense, it is no different to them from taking up the game of chess. They do not see that it is their very lives that are at stake, that they are merely playing with serious things, and that such activities have absolutely no meaning. Only when seen to be something extremely vital, literally a matter of life and death, will a spiritual interest have any meaning to a human being.

The spiritual journey is not only an extremely lonely one but also entails that one is not afraid to be an iconoclast should this become necessary. And in view of the topsy-turvy world view one inevitably arrives at on such a journey, an iconoclastic attitude will necessarily be involved.

The inner need that has driven one towards a spiritual orientation may have resulted from a jolt that one has received, such as a serious crisis in life that has put all

one's certainties in doubt; it may be the result of a pro-
longed period of intense emotional suffering or inner
conflict, or it may somehow result from an unquench-
able curiosity which could be inborn — a need for
knowing that cannot be satisfied with the usual stock
answers given by one's environment. Absent such an
inner need, a foray into the spiritual becomes an
extremely arid, intellectual enterprise. Why should anyone ever get into it? Obviously, if one is not inner-driv-
en one is outer-motivated — i.e., one is influenced by
one's peers, by fads, etc. — and since one's inquiry is not
on the right basis, it can never lead to a truthful answer.
It is also, logically, a situation fraught with contradiction.
The spiritual inquiry is to go deep within oneself in
order to discover how one is ever living on the surface
and how all one's motivations and actions are part of the
collective dream — a mere existence without any
authentic roots in the Self. One is, as it were, fighting the
enemy — which is the world of the false (*Maya*) — at
the behest of the enemy. Now how can such a battle ever
have a different outcome than leaving the enemy
unharmed and entrenched as ever?

But even given an inner need for the spiritual, there
are further difficulties. In our everyday life we are used
to relying almost exclusively on logic, which is the intellectual process, also described sometimes as the linear
thought process, and only very little on our intuitional
capabilities. Now, unfortunately or fortunately, a spiritual truth cannot be corroborated or "proven" by the
process of reasoning. This is because there is a level of

reality that is prior to logic, prior to consciousness with its division into subject and object. However, the subject and object are products of one's conditioning and, therefore, cannot possibly determine the Unconditioned, which is the real. With the birth of the subject and object, a whole world of concepts, suppositions, and theories springs to life, and we are no longer even aware of the real which underlies that thought world. So dominated or "hypnotized" are we by these various projections of the mind that we feel we can discover and define the real through and within thought. But the real will come to us, uninvited; we cannot and need not reach out for it, if only we let go of our frantic mind activity. Thought, unlike insight, is a process that needs time, being based on memory reactivation. A spiritual truth is perceived in a flash, by direct perception, without the thought process having had anything to do with it. Even in science, the really creative breakthroughs have come, initially, as the result of an intuitive revelation, which was only subsequently corroborated by the thought process.

An example of the kind of difficulties one runs into when trying to intellectualize spiritual inquiry is the following. In contemplating the manifested world, no progress in one's understanding can be made until one's vision of the world, and *ipso facto*, one's self in that world, has drastically changed. Instead of viewing the "world" as absolutely real, and therefore, as separate from the equally real "self," with the world imposing its inexorable demands on that self, the Upanishadic seers came up with a different picture. According to them, the world and the self are not really separate, and both are more of an illusion, a dream, than they are solid reality. The rishis (or sages) hit upon the true state of affairs by diving deep within themselves, through which they came to the realization of the Void — which is, essentially, the realization of the "emptiness" of self and the entire manifested world. Here, "emptiness" must be seen as a lack of concreteness, a total relativity, in which nothing is a "given"; *not* as a voidness or vacuum in the nihilistic sense, however. Now there are many texts extant that purport to clarify (or prove) this original insight for the uninitiated by logical argumentation, leading up to a conclusion that the world is not "real." They serve some purpose in making it plausible that things are not as they appear to be (a valuable lesson also learned from the findings of modern physics, especially on the fundamental, subatomic level), but at the same time these writings may well add to the existing confusion. This is because, eventually, as the mind pursues this line of inquiry, one arrives at a paradox. To state anything categorically about the reality of the world, one needs to have a yardstick of reality with which to measure the proposition. And this is clearly begging the question, since we have no such absolute standard, for that yardstick itself would be part of the world; in other words, part of that which is to be proved.

Some people have tried to get over this problem by stating that if the world is not real, neither is it unreal; or, in some sense, it is both real and unreal. Those who have dealt with the problem primarily in an intuitive manner and have seen through it, will understand. Others, who very much depend on verbal statements and logical conclusions through their thought processes, will be all the more nonplussed. Now I think there is a way of bypassing, if not breaking, the impasse. In what follows, and more deeply in the next chapter, I shall elaborate upon an alternative approach of viewing the situation.

Rather than postulating the world to be unreal, I state the world to be *relative*; that is, it depends for its existence on something else. If the world were absolute, it would be an *unqualified* reality; that is, not conditioned, not dependent in any way upon outside parameters, and therefore altogether beyond space and time. But it can be readily seen that the very opposite is the case: the "world" is ever circumscribed by the means of one's observation, by the "observer," where the latter constitutes a set of particular sense organs and brain to interpret and integrate these sensory impressions into a world picture. After all, the world and the observer always stand in a close relationship; they mutually affect each other, so that both are seen to be relative entities, and both are seen to be part of one continuum.

Having come thus far, a further, very interesting, question arises. If that world continuum enjoys an inherently relative existence, there must be something that supports its relative existence. What does that world depend on? It must be clear, and it also follows logically, that the perception of the world as relative entails the necessity of an absolute background. In other words, the postulate of the relative implies *ipso facto* the existence of an absolute. One might also say that the world, the manifest, is permeated by an absolute matrix, the Unmanifest, from which all things — both material and mental — arise and into which all things return upon their disappearance. And, obviously, that is what I am, ultimately and absolutely, and in actuality: the changeless Reality, beyond space and time, and therefore beyond description, beyond definition — the Nameless, the All-Inclusive. So all and everything are within me, the world that I am familiar with as well as the myriads of worlds of the Cosmos. The world no longer has any hold on me, no longer induces fear or greed, no longer urges me on in any way towards my so-called fulfillment, for simply: *I am That.*

27 ≫

A NEW APPROACH TO AN OLD PROBLEM

I once had a discussion with a theosophist lady of my acquaintance on the age-old question of the existence or nonexistence of the world of our experience. To all appearances, her insight was quite penetrating; and, interestingly, she gave the problem yet another twist by seeing the controversy mainly in terms of an East/West antithesis. In the East, the discussion rages over the alleged unreality of the world; in the West its absolute reality is generally taken for granted. The Eastern view leads to paradox and fuzziness, as we have seen (e.g., "The world is both real and unreal."); the Western view is unsubstantiated and therefore meaningless, and blocks insight. Hence, she averred, the whole issue remains inconclusive.

Further to the approach taken in the previous chapter, I think there is a way to bridge the polarized viewpoints from East and West and transcend the entire dilemma through bypassing the controversy of what is real and what is unreal. And I feel the most effective manner to do so is by focusing in on the unquestionable (and demonstrably meaningful) relativity of the world in close conjunction with the nature of the perceiver (or the statement-making entity). If, as we have already seen in the previous chapter, there is ever an intimate relationship between the world and the perceiver of that world, there is obviously no sense in looking exclusively at one or the other.

Much of our difficulty springs from the fact that the language does not accommodate us in such endeavors. The very words themselves already have cut up reality into arbitrary units. Thus, for a start, I would like to examine somewhat more closely the common statement "the world exists." In this context, what is the meaning of the word "exists"? In order to clarify the meaning of this particular term, we are immediately forced to give our full attention to the question "Who is it that says 'the world exists' or that anything exists, for that matter?" After all, that which is to be defined must be considered in close connection with the "definer," for the latter lays down the terms of reference for the process of defining, understanding. If a deaf person tells me he heard some beautiful music or a blind person tells me he saw something extraordinary, and I take their statements at face value without investigating the deafness or blindness of the observer, what value will my conclusions have?

Now any categorical statement that the world exists, in an absolute sense, can be meaningful only if he who says it has absolute existence himself, for obviously for anything that itself has merely relative existence to allege that something has existence, or is *absolute*, is meaningless. For how could the relative know the absolute? Its "knowing" is necessarily restricted to the relative level.

Now to state: "Such and such exists" obviously has a certain meaning, but that meaning is ever valid only for, and restricted within, the context of the maker of that statement. It can never, under any circumstances, have any more universal validity, because in order to have universal validity it should be independent of he who posits it. Now the latter is really only another entity whose existence needs to be proved, dependent upon some further entity that must judge its absolute existence, and the same applies, of course, to that last entity, which in turn needs to be proved, and so on in an endless regression.[1] So what does all this mean? It means that the question of absolute existence of "things" can never have any significance and that the manifested world of "things" is clearly the interplay of a chain of relativities. Our conclusion is not that the world is real or unreal, but that the world is relative.

The same can also be demonstrated in other ways. For example, the sensory nervous/brain system that constitutes the "observer" regards the world as object. But is

1 The reasoning with respect to the reality of the "world" applies analogously to what in the East is called *jiva* (the "individual soul"). The *jiva* is real only to the *jiva* itself and can never be anything other than that. A perfectly circular argument! This writer finds that in any exploration to the most fundamental level any of three things ever happen: the appearance of a paradox, a circular argument, or an infinite regression. In fact, these occurrences seem to afford the best evidence that the inquiry has gone as far as possible. Thus, within the sphere of of duality man can never arrive at any certainties, any absolutes.

not the former itself also part of the world? So how can the observer pronounce on the existence of the observer when it is itself part of the observed? Can the eye see itself? Obviously, it cannot. The observer and the observed are one! This means, in a way, that when examined as separate beings they collapse into one another — as in physics, an electron and a positron cancel each other out upon meeting through mutual annihilation; that is, the result is zero! Or, as Sri Nisargadatta Maharaj has stated, what we actually are is a dimensionless point! Thus, that zero contains everything, both in actuality and as Infinite Potentiality!

The world is inherently the reality of the statement-maker and so is part of the statement-maker. We should never look for it beyond him. In fact, the idea of the world as an outside entity — divorced from the statement-maker — should be given up entirely.

Yet another way to see this is as follows. The absolute nature of the observer as a separate entity is obviously based upon the nature of the body; it stands or falls with the body's absolute or relative existence. In my dream I possess a body that is independent — functioning independently — from my body in the waking state, and "I" have really two bodies, each with entirely different activities. My "dream body" ends upon the ending of my sleep/dream state, when it is seen to be wholly a product of the dramatic capabilities of the mind during sleep. That body and its actions, both so real to me during sleep, are seen upon my waking to be nothing but the product of imagination.

From here, it is not too difficult to take the next step and see that the other body, the body of my waking state, is similarly the product of my sensory/cognitive process, and ends upon the awakening from my waking/dream state. Without the action of thought-memory, the concept of the body is not. Thus, the "body's" existence and thought are ever intimately entwined. In conclusion, when talking about the existence of the observer, it is therefore thought only that talks about him; the observer is real only insofar as "he" is in thought, part of thought — "he" and thought are one. As Krishnamurti puts it: "Thought creates the thinker, not: there is the thinker who produces thought." Or, as the Buddhists say: "All is Mind," and what is at any moment is what your mind makes of it. Beyond it is the Absolute — spaceless, timeless, and ever mysterious because it is beyond the process of observing/knowing. Yet, That we are, and so long as thought is operating, as it usually is, we are, in the deepest sense of the word, alienated from our real nature. And it also follows that our conventional spiritual disciplines and meditation practices necessarily perpetuate and deepen that alienation, for they are essentially predicated upon an absolute world view.

Our entire discussion thus far in this chapter seems to me a glaring example of the limitations of language, of how it ever reinforces the self-enclosed vision of our reality and falsely lends it some absolute foundation. Having seen all this clearly once and for all, we are immediately rotated into another dimension beyond the word, and beyond the verbalizing mind. We have then reached a sphere of silence in which there is immediate clarity far beyond the befuddling effect of the thought-word grooves of the mind. Never again shall we lightly make statements about existence or nonexistence; and the insight brings us back to the starting point of this inquiry. For it is now seen that the very question of whether something exists or does not exist should itself not exist, because it is the wrong question and, obviously, a wrong question can never lead to a valid answer.

28 ⤨

SEEING THROUGH ONESELF

The two previous chapters may have seemed some-what of a philosophical or metaphysical interlude. It may therefore be appropriate to recapitulate our findings and to say a few words in order to link what may appear to be highly theoretical, and therefore actually useless, with the practical art of living without problems.

Whether the world is real or not leads to the paradox that the problems therein may be real or not real, yet in actual fact this does not make the slightest difference to our everyday life. The point is that to those who desig-nate the world as "unreal," the so-called "non-problems" are just as painful in their experience (or, in this context, should one say "non-experience"?) as the so-called "real problems" to others who see the world as "real." Saying "the world is a mere dream" does not make our life any less of a hassle; it does not make our minds less confused and the world less chaotic. And it does not help one iota to make the world into a more peaceful place. One wishes it would be that simple! Such statements are merely exercises in soothing semantics that are far removed from the *actuality* of living through conflict and sorrow. Thus, on the plane of logic — that is, the level of thoughts and words — there is obviously no release from the kind of consciousness that ever embraces us in a stranglehold.

Abandoning, then, this particular, unproductive approach, one is led quite naturally to inquire into the related question of whether the world (and also, the "individual") is relative or absolute. And, as we have already seen, the world and the self, or the observed and the observer, ever stand in a close relationship, in which each is dependent upon the other. This confirms the relative nature of both, neither having an independent identity.

The crucial question now is: Where does this lead us? What is the real meaning of the statement: "The world is relative, the self is relative — neither is ever absolute"? If we take this finding as anything to go by in our everyday life, we are lost; because then we treat the insight as a conclusion, a concept that should be fit into a method, a "how-to" formula for saner living. This would then become part of the thought process via memory — another form of "know-how," and as we have already seen, "know-how" does not work in the spiritual life. Only "know-not" works there, which is really when we do not depend upon thought-memory for living in this world which is an endless morass of problems, conflict and sorrow. When, silently or otherwise, it is acknowledged that we "do not know," the mind gives up looking for a solution to the problem(s) by which it is momentarily beset. Then, when the thought process is in abidance, there is not just a vacant mind, or a vacuity in consciousness, as one might expect through the sheer logic of things. No, in that moment there is an action from beyond the mind, which manifests itself as a state of awareness without an entity that is the initiator of this awareness. In other words, the awareness has no limitations and divisions into the inner and the outer. For, as we have already seen on previous pages, *the entity comes into being only through and within thought.* Therefore, "no thought" signifies "no thinker" or no "I" who is aware. If one is conscious of being aware, one is not aware. One simply thinks about oneself being aware — or, more to the point, one thinks about oneself and therefore gives continuity, and so sustenance, to that thought-created entity.

Now it seems to me that the essential cause of the human predicament is that, instead of being satisfied with the status of his relative existence, man makes himself constantly absolute (i.e., to himself, but not in reality) and, thereby, miserable. This "absoluteness" is, of course, a phony absoluteness. A truly "absolute" state is ever out of reach to the mind, for whatever is in thought must be relative, time-bound, limited. Analogous to what we stated in the previous paragraph, it is merely the relative *thinking* about the absolute, imagining itself to be, not *being it.* The truly absolute cannot be conceived and is not possible within the realm of the Manifest. Thus, it is the false absoluteness that generates suffering.

If "one" is truly relative — that is, fleeting, unsubstantial, or "empty" — then one is never hurt, one accumulates nothing, especially in the way of psychological scars; and life and death become one to such a relative (I think, the only word that fits for noun to follow) "appearance." The opposite way of life, as can be readily seen, is a veritable way of death — a continuous strain to protect one's "absolute" existence — an endeavor ultimately doomed. We shall elaborate upon this subsequently.

Now we must reiterate that the foregoing exercise in unraveling the issue "'Me' — am I relative or absolute?" does not at all serve as the starting point for a new philosophy of life, or another way of functioning, but as such can and must be forgotten immediately. Its utility lies in the fact that the insight provides a marvelous illustration — and therefore facilitates our understanding — of what we are doing to ourselves and why, consequently, we suffer. The point is that *we constantly go against our real nature*, our natural state, when we try to make ourselves into something that we are not — a projected "absolute" condition — like trying on a glove inside out! It does not fit and so we are continually suffering from dis-ease. Through lack of self-knowledge, we do not see that the moment we consider ourselves to be absolute (which is the work of thought upon experience, involving memory), we set ourselves up for a fall. The imagined absolute "me" becomes involved with space and time, leading to fear, greed, desire, and ultimately the experience of suffering through the collision of the "unreal absolute" with the "real relative."

Now there is one more aspect to this marvelous insight of man's relativity that may be found helpful. If I am genuinely in a state of "choiceless awareness" (in the words of J. Krishnamurti) or "'I' am' consciousness" (in the words of Sri Nisargadatta Maharaj), *then I am purely in the state of the relative.* And in that state there is not even a possibility of giving rise to the seed of an absolute "me." This is because one is beyond the mind and, therefore, beyond thought-memory; there is no continuity. There is no time for any problem to persist in and no "me" or "problem-maker" to subsist or persist. There is only the seeing or "witnessing"! The important part is to see that the "absoluteness" of the "me" and the witnessing of what *is* are ever mutually exclusive. Thus, when reverting to thought, or psychological brooding, we ipso facto give rise to the absolute entity that faces the world, worries, suffers, and so forth. And, conversely, when there is pure seeing, without judgment in terms of good and bad, or "what should" and "what should not" be, then that seeing is all there is: ever perceiving fresh facts from moment to moment, without resistance, done by X, as it were — the great Unknown — because it is in the absence of any known, identifiable, persistent-in-time entity.

As long as there is a connection in our mind with any knowledge on the psychological level, there is the formation and/or maintenance of such an entity that we call "myself" and which is considered concrete enough to fight for with all we've got. This connection could be as "attachment" to an idea or image, or even as the state of tension resulting from efforts at so-called "detachment." Let me give an example. We are all in some way affected by public opinion — be it the opinion of the populace (i.e., society) or that of one's mother-in-law or whoever in particular. Consciously or unconsciously, we ever want to be "popular" (which means, fundamentally, conform: "think as the people") or defend our "respectability." So, although strictly legally there are certain limiting parameters for our behavior, underlying it there is a more powerful restraining force at work. Therefore, our actions can never be spontaneous, when they would be infallibly right, but are always the result of mentation, calculation, with a view to maintaining and protecting the various images of oneself that are carried in memory. And it is these images with their untold associations in thought that constitute the only continuity of the self as "entity." In a more general way, it can be said that our actions are ever motivated by gratification of desire in one kind or another. Thus, one is never free but always at the mercy of external circumstances. And if not external, then there are internal factors, such as the many self-created goals that one wants to achieve and the challenges of the various mind games that one plays within and with one's self.

To recapitulate: Upon what one *is* — fleeting, transient, pure relativity — thought has erected a superstructure of knowledge; and it is this artificial, thought-spawned superstructure that affects an "absolute" posture or "persona." It thereby becomes not only a burden but also a source of ever-spreading disturbance in consciousness. Without that superstructure, one is simply what one is: a conduit for experience, the eternal witness which itself consists only of pure witnessing. And since witnessing in its purest form entails no resistance, where then is room for conflict or unhappiness?

Not to go along with all the mind's trickery, through keen alertness in a state of choiceless awareness, is true simplicity; this seeing through oneself is the flame that consumes all that which one is not.

In sum, the insight of man's relativity and the state of being choicelessly aware are, in fact, two sides of the same coin, and the reason we have dwelled upon it to such an extent is that the perception of both these aspects seems somehow to work synergistically towards a deeper understanding of oneself and thereby helps to arrive effortlessly, methodlessly, at the state of consciousness that can deal with this world, come what may. Once this "seeing" has taken place, in a moment or a flash, like a blessing, it can be forgotten. And what is more, it must be forgotten lest it not in itself become some "knowledge" detrimental to the natural fluidity of mind and thereby contribute to the problem of the "I"'s false absoluteness — or, that of *thinking* what we are instead of *being* what we are.

29

To Freeze or Not to Freeze, That is the Question—Or is It?

Recently, a gentleman in California suffering from an incurable brain tumor requested to have his head frozen while still alive. The idea was to decapitate him and preserve the head indefinitely at a very low temperature until such time that a cure for his disease could be found. Then, presumably, another functioning body sans head could be drummed up from somewhere and joined with the head to make him whole again, in some fashion. The courts, however, refused to play along and declined permission to start with the proceedings. Now I am not concerned with the legal niceties of the matter; I am wondering, however: Is this scheme, even if it could be pulled off, really necessary?

Let us suppose for one moment that the experiment succeeds in assembling the body parts in a viable manner, what have we got then? A living functional body that will persist for a period, eventually to succumb to some disease or "old age." Then, if so desired, the process of freezing and joining the body parts can be repeated — and so on, ad infinitum or ad nauseam, depending on the degree of zest for life that the subject can still muster after one or more such life cycles.

However, my interest in all this lies more specifically with the question: Who or what is the subject before the cryogenic phase and who or what is he after the cryogenic phase? For only if I can clearly establish these identities can I be sure that from the subject's point of view it concerns the same person and that therefore the purpose of the operation has been achieved.

Initially, of course, the man has a social identity — call him "Mr. X" for the sake of convenience. But what actually is a "person"? The identity conferred by a "given" name is indeed merely that — literally, an assigned label. To find the answer to this question, one has to look more deeply.

There is in the first place the body, which is constantly changing — with cell tissue building up and breaking down all the time. One might say that "body" is a self-maintaining system comprised of organic matter in a state of dynamic equilibrium. Superficially retaining a certain recognizable form, in reality it changes every moment and over a longer period of time may become unrecognizable. So which body are we talking about?

The issue, however, may be totally irrelevant, because even if the body were unchanging and eternal, are we that body? Are we really only that combination of name and form (*nama-rupa*)? The very fact that we can view the body as an object among many others means that there is a distance between the subject and that body, that we are not it — or, at least, not merely it. The body, as in fact the whole world, is viewed by us as subject, in the capacity of consciousness, and so obviously it is there that the clues as to what we are must be sought.

In the awareness of Beingness, or the light of sentience, and also during its apparent absence such as in deep sleep, have I ever discovered myself as a "person," an enduring entity? From the earliest days of conscious awareness of interaction with the environment, I was busy "experiencing" and accumulating selective experiences as "memory." Eliminating the body image, it seems that nothing exists but a series of impressions of various relationships, a sequence of memories of events, "experiences," but never an actual person that one can get one's hands on. Similarly, desires, fears, and strong emotions in general create certain engrams registered in the brain. It is all these residues which are "named" and stored as memory that create the illusion, the feeling, that there is something unchanging, a "me," a "doer," a "seer." But all that is a concoction of memory. Things are actually in a state of total flux, but memory makes it appear as if they are not, that there are certain entities which are independent in their existence, which endure, and so can be "recognized."

In this way also has come about the illusion of an "I," an individual person. Observing this string of experiences preserved in memory, I say it is "mine," oblivious of the fact that this is a mere inference, a "feeling," not something tangible, actual. The reality is that from the beginning of awareness one has had nothing but experiences and only the vaguest, ever changing concepts and images of an "experiencer" or a "me." This impression is constantly being reinforced by hearsay. Consequently, our thoughts and imagination are feverishly at work to construct, maintain, and beautify the hypothesized entity and then to prescribe certain activities for it. But occasionally when this mental activity slows down or ceases, such as in moments of quiet contemplation or in deep sleep, all that is effaced. Experiencing has ceased for the time being and what is left only is an infinite Emptiness or a state of pure Beingness, completely transparent and devoid of personalities or entities.

Examining further the experiencing entity or "ego" that has been called forth by thought and as thought, we find that it is totally fluid, having nothing permanent to it. For example, in the waking state it may be entirely different from what it is in the dream state. And one may then ask: Which is to be considered the real "me"? The answer, of course, is neither; for only that which never changes can be said to have an identity.

Here it might be objected that notwithstanding all that we have said so far, it appears that we can guide or control the thought flow at will, indicating the existence of some entity, a "controller." In other words, I (that is, a master control) am in charge of the thought process. But then one may further ask: Who is it that decides to activate the "controller"? Is it not itself part of a thought pattern? Furthermore, if the commonly accepted view were correct — that there is a "thinker" controlling his thought, or an "experiencer" controlling his experience, a person asleep would never have a bad dream for the dream experiencer would resolutely step out of it. There would be no mental suffering at all, for the thinker would not allow it; he would actually always live with glorious and pleasurable thoughts. Wish it were so! The reality is that the "guide" or "control" of thought is a deception, it is part of thought itself; the "experiencer" is part of experience itself. It is a mere strand in the network of thought. Just like a wave on a water surface is nothing but water, so the imagined thinker or "I" is but a disturbance in the ocean of consciousness.

Returning now to Mr. X, what will be the situation post-freeze? There are two possibilities. Through the internal hibernation, memories have either been lost or they have been preserved. If lost, Mr. X as such (that is, to himself) is no more; a new pseudo-entity will have to be built up. Strangely, he will be like a newborn baby with a ready-made adult body (somewhat of a freak, I suppose!), and the freezing has been for naught. As to the alternative, memories having been preserved, I think this is extremely unlikely. Even an inanimate tape recording loses its magnetism over time and thereby the information recorded on it, so let alone the much more sensitive organic substratum that is the brain. Furthermore, in living organisms memories are maintained because they are constantly being revitalized — that is, fresh experiences are related by association to ear-

lier engrams, and so memory is being kept alive. Yet, we
cannot be sure how all this turns out; it could be that
like Rip van Winkle, Mr. X simply emerges as from a
long sleep with basically memory of a previous existence
intact. But, in that case, he will probably find that these
memories have little relevance in the changed
(estranged?) world which Mr. X now inhabits. Even the
prevalent vocabulary will be quite alien to him.
(Somewhat similar to an aging person in a very young
environment finding himself "out of it.") And because of
this alienation he will soon forget the basics from his
previous existence and, again like a newborn baby, find
he has to start all over again. In other words, he must
build up a new, subjective "identity" from fresh experiences. Since what passes for "identity" is largely a socially determined product, he will have to die to all the
memories retained from his previous life span in order to
properly "fit in" with his current environment. It might
well prove a somewhat painful transition, this dying to
so many yesterdays — a kind of conscious death process.
Ironically, the intention of evading death, which set off
the entire exercise, may result in an intense encounter
with death. So even in this eventuality, to all practical
purposes, he will no longer be the same as pre-freezing.

Whatever the case may be, with continuity broken in
the manner described, in place of "Mr. X," there will
now be a "Y"— Mr. or Ms. (depending on the trunk
added to the head). Mr. X, divorced from his past, has
disappeared for good. The experiment, even when suc-
cessful, will have failed in its essential purpose!

In the final analysis, we are left with the question: Is all the freezing, cutting, thawing and splicing really necessary? Can it fundamentally achieve its purpose, and are the great costs, risks and efforts involved justified? You see, in the end, what X really is — and we say X purposely without prefix denoting gender, as his real nature is neither male nor female — has not changed at all. That which is X is, actually and timelessly the same as that which Y is: it is the background upon which X, Y, Z, etc. appear, and which itself is not affected by any superimpositions. This constitutes its own continuity — although we are using this term in a very special way — and it signifies the only true Immortality. The key to understanding this is to see through the pseudo-identities assumed and represented.

We can now answer the question heading off this chapter, as we have arrived at the view that the antithesis "to freeze or not to freeze" is not the issue here at all. If Mr. X had really understood his plight, he would do nothing to extend association with the body which has been the cause of his dis-ease and, on a deeper level, the source of all un-ease. He would perceive that it is precisely this continuity in time — and especially the desire for it — which is the problem and that the only true immortality is attained when one simply merges with Being — the beingness which is ever accessible in the Now because it embraces the whole of time into eternity.

30 ⌒

THE DISCOVERY OF IMMORTALITY

Although certain Oriental scriptures talk about "The Experience of Immortality," we wish to find out through our own actual experience whether there really is such a thing as "immortality." Perhaps "experience" is not exactly the right word, for, paradoxically, if immortality is our natural condition, we may not be able to experience it. Immortality would have to be a "steady state," since an intermittent state of immortality is obviously a contradiction in terms. Yet, by logical necessity, immortality could only be experienced against a background of mortality. This is because for perception and recognition — comprising "experience" — to occur, first a condition of duality, as an interface or contradistinction, must be present. Secondly, the perceiver or experiencer has to be greater in scope, more complex or more sophisticated than that which he wishes to perceive and understand. For example, if a drop of water in the ocean were sentient, it would not be able to experience the nature of water, let alone the ocean. Or, to take another example, the mythical "flatlander" of elementary physics books, living in a world of two space dimensions, can never experience our three-dimensional world. But somehow he has the possibility of arriving at the discovery or insight that his flat world is not the whole truth, is a flawed concept because it leads to contradiction and paradox. And with intelligence and sufficient contemplation, he may even come to realize the whole truth — or perhaps we should say, a greater truth — although due to his inherent limitations, it could never be an "experience" in the way that he experiences his "flatland."

Now, in the same vein, Immortality stands for Infinity, and Infinity is fundamentally different; that is, it is infinitely greater than any finite quantity or form. By the same token, Immortality is infinitely greater and more fundamental than mortality. Therefore, mortality, the known, can never experience Immortality, the Unknown, in the way that it experiences the "world." (But Immortality can understand mortality.)

Thus, not only is the "experience of immortality" now seen to be a misnomer and it would be more appropriate to substitute the term "insight" or "discovery," but also our very inquiry itself is fraught with paradox and strictly circumscribed. Only immortal man can discover his true nature; mortal man's inquiry will forever flounder because of his own inherent limitations. Within this frame of reference, let us proceed.

To answer the question whether man is mortal or

immortal, it will first be necessary to explore very deeply the nature of our essential being — not merely that which we *appear* to be — which will become clear only when all that we are *not* has been completely understood and discarded.

At first glance, man appears to be mortal. This seems an evident and highly visible truth. He is born and dies. This apparently indisputable fact is, however, never directly experienced. Birth and death are always observed with respect to others. The "I" never experiences its own beginning and ending — that is, respectively, the moment of conception and expiration. What happens is that consciousness comes upon us in some inexplicable and apparently acausal manner, and expires in a similar way.

A similar thing happens to us when falling asleep and waking up, or at times of fainting ("losing consciousness"). Since during such episodes, we undeniably exist, to simply assert our birth and death on the basis of possession of consciousness is not valid. Thus, existence is not necessarily synonymous with consciousness.

Now, as to the question of self-existence, where does identity enter into the picture? When different individuals are challenged to describe their identities, they will reply "I am male," "I am female," "I am black," etc. In other words, they will enumerate various attributes, all derived from body-mind, and with which they have identified themselves. What all their statements have in common is "I am," and so what all these individuals inherently are, beneath the various labels or superimpo-

sitions, is the awareness "I am" or Beingness — undiffer-
entiated, unidentified, and unidentifiable. That is, on
this fundamental level, there is no separation between
individuals, no extension in space.

Looked at from a different angle: The seer has identified himself with the seen — or, rather, with a fragment
of it — the one body that he calls his own. Had he identified himself, on the other hand, with the totality of the
seen, this fragmentation leading to grotesque distortion
in his understanding of life would never have occurred.
Instead, he would immediately have come to the holistic
insight: "I am the world."

To identify with "his" body goes hand in hand with
another mental process. Onto the "I am" consciousness
appears the "I"-thought, which is the seed of all further
thought. This means all thought essentially contains and
reflects the "I"-thought in holographic manner; that is, it
centers around a self-concept. And, in the absence of the
latter, which is the mainspring of the psyche, the mind
would be quite still. Incidentally, it is this very polariza-
tion of thought, leading to various crystallized thought
patterns, that we call the "mind." Otherwise, there is no
mind at all,[1] only a creative state of Emptiness (not to be
confused, however, with Nihilism), which in Zen is actually called the "No-Mind" state.

Since man has identified himself with the body, a
space-time frame of reference has been created. The birth

1 "When the mind unceasingly investigates its own nature, it transpires that there
is no such thing as mind. This is the direct path for all. The mind is merely
thoughts. Of all thoughts, the thought 'I' is the root. Therefore, the mind is only
the thought 'I'."—*The Collected Works of Ramana Maharshi, Upadesi Saram*, vv.
19, 17, 18, p. 85.

and death of that body logically implies linear thought or sequential vision; that is, things go from here to there, both in time and in space.

Having arrived at the quite extraordinary understanding of the voidness of space and time, one is necessarily led to a further extraordinary insight. This is to see the accepted order — of being born, living in this world, and finally disappearing from it — as quite erroneous. Such a vision would apply to the body, but my real Self has nothing to do with that. This body, along with all others, and in fact, the entire world of objects, exists within me, owes its origin to me.[1] Thus, looking upon myself in the traditional way — being in the world, in my present body, for a limited time, to finally disappear, and possibly repeating the whole cycle in another body, under different circumstances — is actually tethering myself to a false mortality. The truth is: I ever experience myself and the world as "I am," in my present body, or, more accurately, "containing my present body." Seen from the old viewpoint, it may be my nth body of identification but will necessarily be experienced only as "my present body." After all, when considering that body, do I carry with me the feeling of any previous bodies?

It appears then what the distorted view has done is to spread out, unfold, the dimensionless reality of my Being into linear dimensions, displaying a Universe populated by a multitude of creatures. This unfolding is what in Sri

1 Sri Nisargadatta Maharaj states in this connection: "Did anybody exist prior to me? When my Beingness appeared, then only everything else is. Prior to my Beingness, nothing was." (In a discourse on July 9, 1980, as reported in *The Ultimate Medicine*, Blue Dove Press, San Diego, California, 1995, page 119.)

Nisargadatta Maharaj's teaching has been called the "objectivization" of Reality and represents the quality of *Maya* — the manner in which the Unmanifest, or that which exists timelessly, manifests itself in time. To be able to recognize and identify with that reality which lies beyond space-time and the "seen" is to find oneself at last. This is the real Homecoming, which may truly be called the Discovery of Immortality.

31 ⬿

THE OBSERVER IS
THE OBSERVED

Let us go along for one moment with the conventional view that there is a world out there which has an absolute existence, and a body-mind entity that functions as an observation/communications system. Essentially, this system may be represented very schematically as a straight line — a communications channel —at both ends of which important and mysterious transformations take place. At one end the sensory organs and nerve cells "make contact" with what we call "the world" or the "four-dimensional space-time continuum" in which objects are present and phenomena occur. Thus, the "input" terminus senses the attributes of the world and converts the impressions or data gathered into nerve impulses. These impulses, which are complex electrical and chemical changes taking place in the cell material, are conducted along a network of nerve channels to various places in the body and especially to the most developed part of the central nervous system, the brain. There, at the "output" terminus, the impulses are reconverted into the "original"; that is, the world picture which we have taken for granted but is really an everlasting miracle — a creation out of Nothingness. As a "model" for the perception of an existing and autonomic or "absolute" world, the above representation is plausible, and perhaps even persuasive enough. But, we must ask, is it the whole truth?

Let us study the model a little more closely. Apart from the mysterious transformation in the brain, which is beyond any ordinary understanding, there is the following unnerving observation. In order to convey and produce our vision of the world, there is total dependence on the mediation of the sensory organs and the central nervous system, including and especially the brain. At this stage we need not talk of the mind, because the mind in turn comes into play only after the action of its physiological counterpart.[1] Now the key point here is that the somatic mechanism, consisting of the various cell tissues, is in itself also part of the world perceived. Note, therefore, the following cyclic argument: *To establish the existence of the world, I must first assume the existence of the world!* And, because the observation system itself is part of the world, it disproves the notion of a separate, absolute world that can be observed and discussed from the point of view of an

---

1 This logical sequence is also affirmed by Sri Nisargadatta Maharaj: "Whatever experience you undergo, it is the product of Beingness, and Beingness is the outcome of food. From food is derived the body form . . ." *The Nectar of Immortality*, Blue Dove Press, San Diego, California, 1996, p.33.

independent observer. Since the body-mind as the observer is at the same time the "observed," the world is subjective and arbitrary — essentially no different from the world observed in the dream state. Its four-dimensional nature (space-time), which deceives us into assigning it absolute reality, is now seen to be part of the mechanism of "subjectivity." And, if we are correct in this conclusion, what then remains of the (physical) separateness of individuals, let alone our much-vaunted psychological autonomy?

Not being in and of ourselves in the four space-time dimensions, but, on the contrary, giving rise to those dimensions, it follows that to talk about life, death and afterlife is inappropriate; the fact of the matter is that we ever dwell in eternity.

Now there is another area of existence it would behoove us to look into. Simple life forms generally display a relatively simple structure in their nervous systems and neurons. The conventional view is that such organisms have only partial or simplified perceptions of reality. The underlying assumption here is that the more complex the nervous system is, the more closely perception approximates Reality. This argument forms, of course, the accepted basis for man's alleged superiority over other species of living organisms. But in the light of our findings, *a more complex structure of the nervous system simply means a more complex reality — not a more refined perception of reality*, since there is no reality apart from the creature. Now, if the observed is indeed the observer, then any hierarchy of ultimate values based on the development or "evolution" of physiological structure must collapse. Such an insight strengthens our intuition that all life is One, and that beyond the limitations of the pleasure/pain mechanism, which is strongly involved with the nature and texture of the organism's nervous structure, there is the possibility of "compassion" (a feeling of "suffering-togetherness") or love which transcends species' boundaries. But to the extent that we hold to the erroneous hierarchy of values, we live within the walls of the intellect and so shut ourselves off from such love. Animals, in this respect, are less handicapped.

To return to our main discussion, one difficulty which we have bypassed so far is: How does the brain re-create the mind-formed image of the world? And how does the computer-like mechanism of the brain bridge the gap between the digital impulses received, which represent changes in *matter*, and the resulting *consciousness*—the thinking and imagery that can protect and, if necessary, even mend itself? Intuitionally and also because of the very definitions of "matter" and "consciousness," we feel the two are too far apart for the gap to be bridgeable. Therefore it seems to me that the mechanism of perception based on the conventional wisdom in which body and mind, as well as mind and matter, are viewed as separate entities, cannot be true. It would be like considering a computer as being sufficient unto itself, not needing either a programmer or an operator who interprets and understands the data which the machine has spewed out by itself.

Further contemplation of our "model" will lead to one more important insight — possibly the crux of the matter. Information about the "world" acquired by the "observer" is not what it appears to be at first sight. In fact, the "information" about the basic structure of the world must be considered meaningless since it does not allow for any cognitive alternatives. This question of possible alternatives is mandated by the very concept of information. To quote from the entry under "Information Theory" in the *Encyclopedia Britannica*: "Thus, in information theory, information is thought of as choice of one message from a set of possible messages." An either/or set of possible messages (a "binary digit" or "bit" for short, such as the on/off position of a switch) is a minimum information requirement in this respect. In its absence, there is no datum to be transmitted and obviously no possibility of information transmission.

What we are interested in is the very *field of observation*, the background, into which data are perceived; that is, the particular spatiotemporal mode of presentation of objects and events, which appears fixed and is always taken for granted. And also qualitatively: Why should re-creation of the "world" come about through mediation of just the five senses — why not, for example, four or six or whatever?

It is not like looking through a telescope, where the eye has the freedom to observe. We are concerned with what happens behind the eyepiece, in the brain, which has no choice in its mentation of the basic parameters of the "seen." Why is there a background to the field of perception at all? And what and wherefrom is the light that makes the background perceptible? Both background and light do not come from "out there," although they arise at the same time as my Beingness. They are manufactured by the brain itself. In this respect, the brain differs from every other information system. Other systems fulfill the requirement stated above that the information conveyed must represent a choice between alternatives. Now the brain can convey information about objects and events within its predetermined matrix, the basic four-dimensional space-time frame of reference, but not at all about this reference system itself, which is an *a priori* condition. Thus, information may be conveyed about events within the world, on the physical level as well as the psychological overlay, but the underlying physical matrix, the very nature of the reference system in which the events take place, is deterministic. This forecloses any further enquiry into its nature.

A variety of possible answers as to the nature of the "observed" as the fundamental reality underlying all perception might have been possible if the "observer" and the "observed" were truly separate and independent from each other. But this is patently not the case. The observer states there is a four-dimensional (space-time) universe out there, because the brain says so. In this, *the "observed" is the particular way in which the brain comes up with an answer.* One may say, the so-called "nature" of the world is more appropriately indicative of the mysterious transformation mechanism of the brain than of the nature of the world. By the same token, "the nature of the world" loses all conventional meaning as a concrete separate reality. Again, what we are up against is that the answer is already contained in the question. Rather than us observing the world, *we are the world.* So much for the reality of an "absolute" world that may be known and defined! Our conclusion must be that *there is no ultimate ontology.* Not only is obtaining an ultimate knowledge of "what is" not possible, but also the very idea of there being such knowledge must be given up. This answer may perhaps not satisfy many who are accustomed to the Western philosophical tradition but will not be too surprising to those familiar with the sages of the *advaita* tradition who maintained that ultimate reality can never be known since it lies totally beyond any subject-object duality; rather than "know" one must *be* That. Implied in this is also the insight that all "knowledge" as such is limited, confined within the body-mind sphere. Man, through knowing, experiencing, thinking and feeling, can never break out of the prison of his body-mind. This at once indicates the necessity for a letting go of this entire realm of the mind — of pushing oneself, through thinking, toward some conclusion about the Ultimate — for all such thinking is fundamentally flawed, it being circular in nature. Yet, the intelligence that can look upon this confining body-mind sphere realizes *ipso facto* its own otherness from it, and so enjoys a taste of absolute Freedom. Also, to see the futility of one's habitual efforts immediately ends them and allows the possibility of the Other — the being and realizing of what *is* — to take place spontaneously.

So, how must we evaluate then the brain's perception? Its perception must be viewed rather as an imprint on something else (the Real), but in which the imprint, because of its own unreal, dreamlike nature, is more like a rainbow in the sky. Being totally determined, the "answer" given by the brain is of the nature of a physiological reaction. In fact, it is totally that. One might also say that the most profound activity of the intellect is still essentially mechanistic. The observer might as well say "blah, blah, blah," it would not make any difference. Whether the observer "finds" there is a four-dimensional world out there or a ten-dimensional one, what does such a statement actually mean? It means only that a psycho-physiological or "cognitive" movement takes place which comprises an "observer-observed" continuum whose stirrings result in a mere "static" or "noise" inherent in that continuum. There is also the revelation that the notion of there being a "world" (which fundamentally implies the existence of something discrete, of absolute reality, and that can therefore be "named") is erroneous and must be abandoned. We might say with equal validity that all is the "observer" as that all is the "observed," which is another way of saying, *there are no boundaries* (as all so-called "boundaries" are arbitrary and mind-posited). Thus, the consciousness or intelligence that can discuss these matters is what we are — which is the self from which everything and every activity flows. That which has no boundaries and is unnameable has been termed the "Void," although this is a mere code word for something that eludes any kind of description or verbalization. Being outside space-time — that is, Infinite — means that it is the Whole, invulnerable, and immortal.

32

ETERNITY IS EVER NOW

The cause of man's spiritual dis-ease — our identification with the body — has been amply investigated and confirmed. But, it seems to me, we must retrace the diagnosis one step further and ask ourselves: What really is that body which serves as the underpinning for the "me"? Is that body fundamentally "real"? Once we have asked those questions, they must be seen to be inseparably connected with another, even more basic question: *To whom* is that body "real" or "unreal"? That question reaffirms the old dictum that without knowledge of the perceiver, the self, no problem can be approached in a meaningful and fruitful way. Without such self-knowledge, we are doomed to go around and around in circles, and all "answers" will only throw up further questions.

The body brings with it its own special and limited consciousness — seems to envelop it, as it were. This consciousness is totally dependent upon, and the product of, the body's sensory functions. Commonly called the "mind," or the "ego-consciousness," it acts like a center to protect and foster the body's interests. This activity then extends itself, creating a psychological dimension as the more general "body-mind" sphere of interest. In this is created not only a physical, but also a psychological separation, commonly experienced as the "me" versus the "you."

Now everything that is perceived, experienced, understood, interpreted and felt is done so by the body-mind entity, and by nothing else. This is logically, inescapably so. The content of man's consciousness is totally within the sphere of body-mind. Therefore, it is the body — or more accurately, "body-mind" — that is examining the reality of "body," and can such an enquiry have a meaningful answer? If the answer is "yes, the body is real," this signifies only that the body affirms its own reality — according to the yardsticks of reality that only the body possesses. Is it not like saying: "I exist, because I say so"? But a denial, "Body does not exist," would be equally meaningless once the entire process has been understood correctly as a kind of special pleading, or a circular argument. At this point, one may well ask: "Who is it that understands the process correctly?" It is still only body-mind, of course, but this finding spells the emasculation or silencing of body-mind. This leads to a transcendence from which emerges the fact that "body" is essentially the product of its own projection, the expression of its own limitation or basic Ignorance. With (and from) that body comes the "world" of our experience, which springs likewise from that primordial self-projection.[1] Thus the "me" and the "not-me" are swallowed up by the Void, and all our challenges, desires and fears are now seen as self-projected. But because this process of self-projection remains unrecognized for what it really is within this internal self-projection, mental tribulations appear and are experienced as very real. And mental suffering can only continue so long as identification with the self-projected entity persists. Our conclusion then is that identification with "body" is tantamount to identification with a mirage. Space and time come about only through and with "body." If we are not the body, we are the Void which has produced the various mirages but in itself is timeless and spaceless. The idea of the before, now, and after is as much part of the mirage — it spells the end of our linear thinking as the rock of our existence. What is called "Eternity," an infinitely long time period, is ever Now, an infinitely short time period only. Our real nature is Immortality, for what is called "death" is the disappearance of something that never had any real existence in the first place. What *is* does not even acknowledge "life" and "death" as mutual exclusives. My true "I am" is birthless and deathless.

---

1 The point is driven home also by asking oneself the impossible question: "What would the world look like if we had six or more sense organs instead of the existing five?" It is impossible to think on the matter because our very thinking is determined and limited by body/mind and therefore ultimately amounts to a circular argument—like all discussions on the nature and reality of the "world." To describe, or think of, the "world" is ever in terms of the five senses only!

33

LIFE, DEATH, AND REINCARNATION

After having examined in depth various fundamental matters — and all such issues are ever closely interrelated — is it now possible to put the questions of death, the fear thereof, and reincarnation in proper perspective?

We have seen that space and time occur only in the body-mind sphere, the unfolding phase of the enfolding-unfolding Universe. We are using the latter term here in the sense that David Bohm uses it and, which, it seems, is essentially the equivalent of Sri Nisargadatta Maharaj's concept of "objectivization" of Reality. Thus, space and time are real as internal issues — that is, within the domain of *Maya* — but are totally unreal without that domain. Therefore, one who has fully understood this is no longer "afflicted" with "life" and "death," and the fear of either or both. One might say that the fear of death is the fear of losing continuity. But this continuity — which derives from Time — has never been real in the first place, has always been imaginary (literally, a question of being based on images, which are memories).

Now what, in this context, could Reincarnation be? Antagonists argue that reincarnation cannot be a reality because there is no self; thus, there is nothing (i.e., no-"thing") that could possibly recur. But whatever may be the truth, the argument is patently false. If there is no self, what am I then at present? I cannot very well deny my own existence, for this very denial is predicated upon it.

I am an *apparent* individuality, a proposition with which, at a minimum, most of us will agree. Now, there is no logical reason preventing that apparent individuality from re-emerging in a continual recycling process. I think this conclusion adequately disposes of the argument.

But the real clincher in all this, the overriding insight, is that both antagonists and protagonists of reincarnation have missed the point. Let us for a moment assume that the reincarnationists are right in their world view. Because there is no real continuity, but only the deceptive feeling thereof, what is the "I" that has reincarnated? Even within my present lifetime, am I not now an entirely different entity from what I was as an infant, an adolescent, a young adult, and will be as an elderly man? Any identity of these individuals is merely incidental —through name, sex, property, profession, etc., which are all artificial labels but do not touch upon the real "self." So if I cannot clearly identify myself while in my present life, how could I possibly do so when I return? The answer is, of course, that I cannot. Were it otherwise, I would now have a memory of, at least, my most recent past existence. The majority of people have no remembrance of such past lives. As to the minority who claim otherwise, their claims have not proven out when checked for veracity. But even if one day evidence were found to stand up to scrutiny, would it change anything in the human condition? It would prove only the reincarnation — or here, perhaps, a more appropriate term is "recycling" — of empty body-mind entities ("empty," because they have no real substance). The Self, on the other hand, does not need to reincarnate, for it exists timelessly.

In practical terms, reincarnation means only that there are memories of worldly experiences in previous bodies in addition to those in the present body. What difference does that make to the quality of our lives? What bearing has it got on the ending of suffering? The "fact" of reincarnation would leave intact the need for self-transcendence as much as ever. It is not "reincarnation" that matters but the belief therein, our clinging to memory (time), that keeps us to our "limited" stature and establishes us as "mortal" beings.

We must see beyond all that. Much of our problem stems from the mixing of two levels, that of *Maya* and the Real, which have not even got any point of contact. Bodies appear and disappear in the now. Owing to the illusion of a Universe that has unfolded into space-time from the dimensionless Infinity, we see "body" — a multiplicity of bodies; through the unfolding of "time," these bodies appear and disappear. Having as much reality as our perception of the Indian rope trick, all this has nothing to do with my real Self, which is That in which all this activity — this coming and going of bodies and objects — is observed but which in itself remains unaffected and is, therefore, immortal.

34

MAN, A SELF-DETERMINED AND SELF-CONDITIONED ENTITY

Although man thinks he has free will and can control the course of his life, the opposite is actually the case. Man, as "body-mind," is a mere machine; beyond that he is God — unlimited, Infinite.

Through Ignorance most of us think we are nothing more than "body-mind" — this is our fundamental hang-up and goes totally unquestioned. And the mind's nature is such that it actually becomes that which it has accepted wholeheartedly. Thus, it never dawns on us that we might be something infinitely greater than our apparent manifestation. In other words, we are at present what we ourselves define and limit ourselves to be! In slightly different terms: *All our thinking is essentially circular in nature.* In any fundamental investigation, this is something we should never lose sight of. And the self-actualizing capacity of mind makes it into a very dangerous instrument. *What it holds true has a good chance of coming true.* Thus, not infrequently one's worst fears are realized and one's fervent prayers are answered!

The notion of human beings as totally "self-determined" is particularly relevant in the emotional sphere—the area of likes and dislikes, hopes and fears. The fact is that *man desires those things he at one time decided to desire.* (There is no "desirable" thing, as such, apart from the entity that "desires.") He is "turned on" by certain things that, he was given to understand, "ought to" turn him on. And, by the same token, he is "turned off" by things that are meant to turn him off, giving rise to his dislikes and fears. (The mechanical metaphor of "turning on/off" is particularly telling in describing the reactive character of man — you push the right buttons and you get certain expected responses.)

Thus, in acting according to his likes and dislikes, man is not really making judgments on the things liked or disliked, but is activating his interior clockwork mechanism of "reactivity," his personal acculturation. This process is an ongoing one, although the most basic layers of conditioning were laid down at some early stage of the individual's development. This happens when Society (in the form of his environment) presents him with a set of alternatives of varying degrees of "desirability." At that point, the highly impressionable subject, not fully conscious of the situation, is sold a bill of goods into the bargain. Then, once a certain conviction has taken root through the mind's ready acceptance and by being caught off guard as it were, a pattern of conditioning is established. Henceforth, it is simply a matter of repeating the pattern, automatically. Tragicomically, the process is completely mechanical; man blames others for his conditioning, yet it is essentially self-conditioning.

The self-determined nature of man is well illustrated by his fanatical political and religious beliefs, for which he is too often prepared to kill his fellow-man, and the various Gods he worships. He is beyond the pale of reason; unfortunately, there is no ground one can build on; there is no such thing as an "open mind." The latter is a contradiction in terms, since the conditioning ever comes with the territory (of the mind), except perhaps in the case of the very young infant or the idiot. The mind abhors a vacuum; it must immediately cling to some concept. Thus, there is no alternative but to undo the mind, return to No-Mind; the strands of self-enclosure that come with body-mind must first be completely unraveled before there can be any freedom.

35

THE ULTIMATE TRANSCENDENCE OF THE BODY-MIND SYSTEM

The universal identification of man with the body-mind entity that he constantly perceives is based on the view that this entity is something substantial, real, for nobody would want to identify with something that is empty, void and so of no inherent worth. Through this identification, man is no longer the Totality but a mere fragment, and all his troubles start.

One key element that can be instrumental in man's awakening from his unconscious state, this unawareness as to his real nature and role in the general scheme of things, must surely be the realization that as a body-mind entity he constitutes a closed system. By that expression we mean that whatever perceptions and truths present themselves to man, they are essentially of his own making, the product of his own being. One becomes increasingly aware of this by following Sri Ramana Maharshi's approach of *vichara* or self-inquiry. This approach consists primarily in constantly asking oneself "Who am I?," "Who is the entity that is thinking, acting, suffering, desiring, etc.?" And I have found it helpful to ask additionally the question, "To whom is the world-experience happening?," which implies, "What is the nature and meaning of that experience?"

So when, for example, the mind takes itself for real, and as a result identification with the body-mind entity takes place, the process must be challenged by asking, "To whom does the mind appear real?," and the answer can only be "to itself, of course"; the mind is real, non-empty only to itself, to the mind, which is like saying "blah, blah, blah." It has the same validity as the thief's statement: "You can trust me, I am honest!" Look who is saying it!

The nature of the mind, which has sprung forth from the body — itself inert and the product of the five elements and the three *gunas*[1] and therefore bereft of any identity — is under examination as to its ultimate nature and whether it possesses any autonomy, any identity. Now how can any such identity ever be confirmed by itself? It needs an outside, more comprehensive, more fundamental reality than itself to do so, and

1 I felt it entirely appropriate to use the terminology of the Upanishadic lore in this context. There, the "five elements"—earth, water, fire, air and ether— are considered to be the fundamental building blocks of the physical universe. (In passing, it may be noted here that these five elements comprise no less than the one hundred plus elements of modern science.) The three *gunas*—*sattva* (purity, clarity, harmony), *rajas* (passion, energy, activity) and *tamas* (inertia, resistance, darkness)—are the basic attributes or qualities that underlie and operate the world process.

the latter can come into play only when the mind has given way, become totally silent. Then this more fundamental Awareness can prevail which shows the total non-identity, the emptiness or insubstantiality of what is called "mind."

In some more detail, this process of self-discovery — or more accurately, "mind"-discovery — takes place as follows. When the thinking process has slowed down, it becomes possible to give attention to individual thoughts. One finds that the mind is always disturbed and pained by those thoughts that revolve around the twin poles of desire and fear. Thoughts of this particular kind are not random in content, but are patterned around a particular construct of body-mind, or name and form, which in itself is not real but consists of the memories of images and concepts that have sprouted from the original "I"-thought. Being only memories, they are purely the reliving or reactivation of the past. The "I"-thought, in turn, has come about when the "I"-am-ness" or Beingness-Consciousness was implanted or superimposed on what one is and was before there was any stirring of thought. It initiated my being aware of my "self" as a separate entity through a process of sensory delusion or *Maya*, and thereby set in motion the entire world process. And because the mind is nothing but the elaboration of that "I"-thought, it is built upon the same false basis of separateness; that is, this "self-awareness," which has had such far-reaching consequences, is essentially nothing more than a false sense of separateness, of seeing and sensing a fragment, where in actuality there is none, where there is only the Whole, in a way that is similar to seeing a snake in the rope. This false seeing and sensing further escalates the mere "separateness" into imaginations of uniqueness or individual identity, whereas in fact the only identity that anyone or anything ever has is that of the Totality.

Finally, in such meditation the mind is seen for what it is — a never-ending whirling-around of memory images and their projections, in purely mechanical fashion. The observation of all this, as from an outsider's point of view, has worked a drastic and strange change in the consciousness, because for once one has stopped fueling the mind's "mindless" (i.e., mechanical, automatic) activities. By non-interfering, there has been interference!

Then also it is seen that there is nothing more to the mind, that all it is is this everlasting elaboration of the "I"-thought — but for that it is completely transparent and so really nonexistent — and therefore that every statement the mind makes is colored by that "I"-thought. In other words, any pronouncement that the mind makes about reality is based upon unreality, any utterance about Truth starts with a lie.

Through such stepping out of one's normal state of consciousness — by transcending the closed system that of itself can never come to the truth — any identification with body-mind is naturally dissipated.

When the false identification is broken, man, although physically and intellectually still a closed system, has realized his potential for being, spiritually, an open system; that is, he is grounded in the Absolute.

Once such grounding has taken place, he is no longer just a fragment, isolated and insecure, and in eternal conflict with other unreal fragments; he has returned to the Totality from which he sprang and which even now is his real home. Being complete within himself, what is there for him to want or to fear any longer?

36

KNOW YOUR BEGINNING

If one wants to understand anything, it helps greatly to know how it has come about — i.e., its source and development. This is because, in a way, the object considered cannot be more than its source or seed, for if it were so, something would have been created out of nothing. For example, the acorn is the oak tree in an enfolded form. Thus, to understand what the body-mind entity is, we must understand its source — what Nisargadatta Maharaj calls the "child-consciousness." Ultimately, this has come about as the result of the merger of male and female fluid essences, forming the beginning of the body that is the substratum of the subsequently developing "I-am-ness" or consciousness.

Thus, from this initial "wetness" has sprung the "individual" and, in fact, the whole world.

Now again, on a different level, one can see how "wetness" is, if not entirely primordial, then a very basic principle to our manifestation. The cells of the central

185

nervous system, like other body cells, consist largely of protoplasm, which is a fluid consisting of about 90 percent water, and so a form of wetness. These cells or this wetness thus give rise to the "I-am-ness," the consciousness or Beingness, which in and of itself gives rise to the whole world of concepts, including those of "wetness," "dryness," "softness," "solidity," etc.

Now see how man is a closed system: any concept is self-generated, but how through this very meditation we have transcended all concepts! A purely mechanistic process, of physiological-biological nature, has produced the living cell which has given rise and sustains the consciousness through which the world has become manifest.

On a deeper level still, going from the cellular level to the atomic and subatomic levels, we know that the familiar concepts from the sensory level no longer apply, and matter has become a form of "emptiness" both as subatomic particles and as the space between these particles. Yet it is this "emptiness" or "nothingness" which gives rise to this whole world of manifestation. One of the things that follow from this is that all explanations are, in a sense, irrelevant and secondary. The world comes about as if by magic. Even to say that the body has given rise to "I-am-ness" or Beingness — as though it were a simple cause-effect relationship — is only an approximation, an accommodation to our habitual linear thought and conceptualization. For, as the Indian thinkers Nagarjuna and Nisargadatta have demonstrated so clearly, the highest truth is that causality — the idea that there are single causes resulting in single effects — is a fallacy, and that at any one particular moment the whole Universe is involved in the appearance of a single event.

Now if indeed the world has come about as if by magic, how can anyone take that world seriously? And how can anyone rationally cling to that apparition?

Our functioning in the world is necessarily as a body-mind entity, and takes place within innumerable frames of reference, each of which contains certain relationships that have validity within that particular frame of reference. The frames of reference are our worldly relationships, the relationships of relative truths. Individually, the frames of reference have significance in relation to each other, but collectively their value is void. Collectively, they are not grounded anywhere, so they are like clouds in the sky or images in a dream.

37 〜

ABOUT THE REALITY OR UNREALITY OF REALITY

Is there such a thing as Reality and what is its meaning? First, we have the "word," then behind that is the concept denoted by the word; then there is the "impression" of the world in my consciousness, without which the "word" would not have arisen; and, finally, there is the question whether behind the "impression" there lies an objective, solid Reality which has an absolute existence — that is, it is not merely something that differs from observer to observer and is therefore a purely relative thing, not deserving of the grandiose title "Reality."

We must begin, I think, to investigate the "world" about which we only know through the impression it has left on our consciousness. That must be the first logical step, as without the imprint on the consciousness the question would not have arisen at all. Now when one looks at the world, the more one examines it the more one finds that there is no independent validation for its existence. The only basis that it has is the mind. In this connection, the first thing one notes is that the world comes into being at the same time that the "I-am-ness," the Beingness, comes into being. The moment one becomes conscious, the world comes into view. And as soon as this consciousness leaves, for example in a swoon or when dreamlessly asleep, everything is gone. So always the "I-am-ness" and the world arise at the same time and go out at the same time. The two are, in fact, one.

Now if I ask myself, is this world that I observe real, perhaps it might be useful to consider the following analogy. Look at a TV screen. One sees the world through the TV and it appears to be real, but of course, we all know better. The TV "production" is a mere reproduction of reality, and very cleverly done! And the interesting thing is that in our natural observation of the world, one apparently finds a very similar mechanism. That world has also been projected — through the medium of the senses and the brain. In the same way that the TV scene—both vision and sound — has been produced through the medium of video cameras, microphones, cathode ray tube, etc., so the reality that we observe has been put together by the senses and the brain. Thus we get the appearance of the "world." But there is just one little detail to spoil this perfect analogy: it is that the brain which is a necessary link in the chain of production is itself part of the world, the end product. So how can this be? To me, the answer to this riddle is that there must have been something wrong in our original assumptions, since causality at this point has ineradicably broken down. The impasse seems to suggest that the worldly picture that we observe is not real at all; it is no more than a dream, an illusion from the very start!

As I have seen through the illusion of the television and know that the TV is a mere *re*production of reality, so I may be inclined to say, that by the same token, the world that I perceive through the medium of the sense organs and the brain is a reproduction of Reality. But on closer consideration, I see that this is incorrect, for paradoxically *the reproduction in this case is the Original*! So what then is Reality, what is the world? I have now arrived at the following insight: Rather than saying that the world perceived is a reproduction of Reality, it is actually a production of my senses and brain; the world is not at all the solid, tangible reality "out there" that most people think it is but is self-generated — both on the physical and psychological levels. Not surprisingly perhaps, I have rediscovered the old *advaitic* truth: self and world are one, or: the observer is the observed.

This meditation runs parallel to considering the paradoxical, cyclical events in the following sequence: sensory data about the world are converted into digital data— that is, nerve impulses — and conducted to the brain where these data are converted into an analog picture of the world. The trouble with this simplistic sketch of a *modus operandi* is that the sensory organs, the central nervous system and brain that are links in this origination chain are themselves part of the world. So what we have here is a chicken-and-egg type of proposition! In other words, to become aware of the world I need the prior existence of the world. So the self in order to generate the world needs the presence of the world in the first place! To this riddle there can only be one answer. The world has no existence separate from the observer: the observer is the observed; so it is not possible for the world to come into being after the observer, nor prior to the observer, but only simultaneously with the observer. And this is, as we have seen, the exact situation that prevails.

From this it further follows that all "explanations" — which always involve a causal chain — are redundant, in the sense that they are not the final truth. (Other examples of such "explanations" are the theory of reincarnation and the theory of evolution.) Ultimately, the world and self come into being as if by magic, in an instant, and are therefore their own cause. In the literature on the philosophy of *Advaita*, this is known as the "Truth of Non-Becoming" (*Ajati-Siddhanta*). It is to be understood that mind has an inherent magic power (*Maya*), whereby the one Self, the one Reality, appears as manifold, giving rise to the world appearance in the process. But with dreamless sleep all that disappears and unicity once again reigns supreme. Sri Ramana Maharshi summed it all up powerfully: "There is no mind, nor body, nor world, nor any one called the 'soul'; One alone exists, the pure, calm, unchanging Reality which has no second, and no becoming." (*Sri Guru Ramana Vachana Mala*, Verse 20, 21).

Now what is Reality? The "objects" of the world, because they are self-generated and perceived by "entities" that are dependent upon their genetic nature and individual conditioning, are relativistic, never Absolute, since the Absolute depends only on itself. So there is no Absolute upon which the world picture is based. Therefore, whatever one observes cannot be the Real — a conclusion that most of us will find hard to accept.[1] But it must be realized that one of our main difficulties here is linguistic. The very word "Reality" suggests something tangible, concrete. Our whole Western thinking is colored by this idea. It is well typified by Kant's "Ding-an-sich," which contrasts sharply with the statement by the sixth patriarch of Chinese Zen Buddhism, Hui-neng, "From the beginning not a thing exists." And even in Plato's myth of the cave dwellers who are mistaking the shadows on the wall for Reality, that invisible Reality is still conceived as something essentially manifest that, if not perceivable by the senses in a direct manner, then somewhere has a concrete existence in its own right and may be perceived or conceived of, at least by inference, after allowance has been made for certain distortions.

More and more Western thinkers are beginning to see the complexity of the mechanism of perception, that what we think or expect to perceive is ever interfering with what we actually perceive. In other words, mental patterns or models are the filters through we see Reality. A good example is Ralph Strauch, whose admirable book *The Reality Illusion — How We Create the World We Perceive* (currently out of print with Station Hill Press, New York) does a fine job explaining such mechanisms

---

1 Compare this also with a statement made by Sri Nisargadatta Maharaj, in a discourse on July 10, 1980: "That which you know, which you can perceive with your eyes, is not true." *The Ultimate Medicine, op. cit.* p. 115.

and their ramifications. And he gives several interesting examples of how social and cultural factors play an important part in the perception — or should one say, "creation" — of our reality. But even here, unless I misunderstand the author, one gets the feeling that beneath it all the existence of an objective Reality is assumed. Few people indeed have seen fully through the reality illusion on its most fundamental level, and have come to the insight that a manifest Reality does not exist, is a contradiction in terms, just as it is a misnomer to talk about an "expression of Reality," since there is no Reality to be expressed. There is only "expression" (what in Zen is called the "Suchness"), or stretching it a bit, one may say that Reality *is* the expression, with the understanding that there lies nothing behind the expression. Every other way of seeing things gives rise to a false duality and contradicts the truth of *Advaita*.

38

ADVAITA (NON-DUALITY)— THE ULTIMATE TEACHING

The teaching is ultimate because there is no further teaching beyond it; it is the end of the road. It is the apotheosis of an inner exploration — a profound insight expressed in words. It is complete. It is total revolution in the psyche, beyond which no transformation is necessary nor possible. It is the total ending of all philosophies, systems, techniques — which, however exalted, are all fragmentary views, and therefore cannot bring about real, fundamental change in the psyche.

The ultimate teaching is the seeing of the entire world in not even a grain of sand, but a single point — and a point that is dimensionless. That mystical "point" then serves as the entry into an entirely new dimension — the world of the truly spiritual and not what in popular parlance masquerades under that term.

However, for the individual embracing this ultimate teaching, the vision of the non-duality of reality does not mean that he has arrived. On the contrary, it is a mere beginning and the understanding has to be constantly tested in life's experience, so that each moment is a new reality. This process of learning, from moment to moment, is a never-ending movement. But without that vision of the wholeness of things nothing is of avail; we cannot even begin to travel on the spiritual path. The intellect reigns supreme, and its inherent fragmentary vision ever throws up new questions, arguments, and doubts.

As an example of such obfuscation by the intellect, a person suggested to me the other day that in actual fact no one has thus far been able to prove conclusively that the ego could not really exist as something absolute, and therefore man's present divisive ways, based on the "you" and the "me" — the cause of all conflict and sorrow — would be vindicated. One had the feeling that in saying this, he was looking for an argument in validation of his present way of life and getting him off the hook in making a complete change from his ego-centered ways. I told him that the most effective manner to find out for himself was to see directly into the Void and recognize the emptiness of the "persona."

I also mentioned that one cannot prove or disprove anything in the spiritual life, that proof is only on the level of concept, the intellect, and that whatever is proved in this fashion could not be a spiritual truth. But overriding this whole argument is a statement made by the late Sri Nisargadatta Maharaj that even if one were to accept such a dualistic world outlook — and there are certain Hindu thinkers who hold to that — there would be nothing wrong with such duality as long as it does not give rise to conflict. There can be divisions without separation, or opposites without opposition, and in that case "duality without conflict" amounts to the same thing as non-duality in its effect on the psyche.

39

A TURNED-AROUND LIFE

What are the implications of the shattering insights of non-duality in everyday living? First of all, being the Self, one is complete in oneself — which means there is no longer any psychological dependency on others for one's fulfillment; in fact, there are no others. And the same goes for "things," since all things exist only in and through the Self. Being the Self, I am naturally alone: there is no longer the division between the inside and the outside, which eliminates all possibility of an outside threat and therefore there is an end of fear — for fear can exist only in duality.

Second, the question of survival, which has been a main directing force in one's life, is now no longer of any importance. Psychological survival is seen to be the survival of a chimera, a mere dream, and therefore the urge for it drops away quite naturally. Similarly, on the physical level, it is no longer important that one should live long. When one is no longer within the body's skin, as it were, no longer identified with its name and shape, the body's life no longer has the relevance it used to have.

Whatever happens to the fictitious entity which we considered to be the "me," whether in the nature of flattery or insults, is no longer carried over in memory. Happenings on the worldly level have acquired the nature of pure theater, to be watched with interest but at the same time with total aloofness — which means the experiences of one's own "me" have not an iota greater importance than those of other "me's," and vice versa. Thus, one never takes sides in conflicts — in the sense of emotional identification with a particular point of view— which we currently do since we are ever motivated by our own vested interests. There is a full acceptance of things as they are at any particular moment. But, with it, there is a realization that things will inevitably be different in the next moment. Life is fluid, but the mind prefers the status quo, which, it thinks, represents security.

Then, also, one has the feeling of not belonging anywhere in particular, and therefore, paradoxically, being at home everywhere. One does not dwell in any particular point in time or space; one feels to be barely in the world, yet there is an extraordinary sense of presence. Since only Being matters, the doing has become correspondingly less important. The nature of one's activities proceeds according to whatever demands and needs present themselves; and the continuous exercise of choice as in life currently being lived has been replaced by a natural flowing with the events. Happiness is always there, regardless of everything; one does not have to do a thing in order to reach it, and there is not even any reaching for it. And, finally, one lives in a world of Silence; the noise of one's own chattering mind has been turned off and that of others is deflected.

40 ❧

QUESTIONS AND ANSWERS

(This chapter is a record of certain questions and answers that came up during private discussion meetings held in California. They are reproduced here in the belief that they may be of wider interest.)

Q: *Am I really the Noumenon, which comprises the entire Universe and is itself Infinity?*

A: What else could I be? The alternative would be to deny my own existence, which simply cannot be done! Is it not amusing to contemplate how we have identified ourselves with the phenomenal, which is the unreal, and thereby have alienated ourselves from our real nature, which is the noumenal? But to see the unreal as the unreal, the phenomenal as a mere appearance, means that I am the real, I am that in which appearances and disappearances manifest themselves. I am the ever-luminous screen upon which the world process is being projected.

Q: *My psychosomatic apparatus is 20 years old, my name is A. F., and I live in Austria. I have studied many religions and sects (Taoism, Buddhism, Hinduism, Islam, Christianity, Zen, Chassidism, etc.) but nowhere have I*

found such power, authority and clarity as in the book I Am
That *by Nisargadatta Maharaj. Since reading him, I try to
obey and follow his advice. Please, Mr. Powell, can you
write me some wise words on how you put Maharaj's teachings into practice?*

A: After your studying such a wonderful text by this
great Master, what could I possibly add for your edifica-
tion? I would suggest you read and re-read Maharaj's discourses until you fully understand them, at the very least
intellectually. By itself, such understanding is nothing,
but without having that first as a solid backing, one cannot very well proceed beyond the intellect. Once you
have such basic understanding, the moment will come
that you will have had your fill of mere reading. You see
that living the teachings is quite another matter and infinitely more difficult. Then put aside the books for a
while. Books also can become a hindrance and an excuse
for staying on the level of the mind and procrastination.

Always bear in mind that whatever you observe,
desire, fear, etc. is only the product of the mind's eye
and does not really exist as such. It exists only as
thought, and is within your self, not without. These are
all the mind's projections, and so essentially there is
nothing to desire, fear, etc., for the Self is ever fulfilled
and all-encompassing. How can it be threatened, when
all is Itself? But if one does not know the Self (which is
man's basic Ignorance), one will ever be taken in and
pushed around by thought, for obviously the mind will
continue to project desires, fears, etc. *ad infinitum*. So

there will be an unending series of things to desire, fear, etc., keeping the turmoil and mental suffering alive. A pointer to the fact that this need not be so is the deep-sleep state, when none of this wasteful and pernicious activity is going on: there is only Bliss, because then the mind is temporarily quiescent. By contemplating these aspects of our existence, one may come to understand the process of basic Ignorance (*avidya*). One wakes up to the falsity of one's separateness or "individuality," and that there is only Consciousness, which is our Self, and perceives how the mind has initially created the "inner" and the "outer" through identification with the body. Never to let any desires, fears, etc. pass from one's attention without seeing how they originate from the false schism of the "me" and the "not-me" is to put the teaching into practice.

In the beginning you will find that in doing so the psychosomatic machinery is very refractory. It is best "controlled" by leaving it severely alone. For by taking it seriously, one assigns absolute reality to it. Even to state "*my* psychosomatic machinery" implies identification and constitutes the beginning of bondage. Just watch the mind flow choicelessly and realize that you, in your real Self, are other than all that — stay scrupulously unidentified and uninvolved. Just be the Witness, and you are only one (unreal) step removed from the Absolute.

Q: Why has Reality placed man in this painful and troublesome situation vis-a-vis Maya, from which he can extricate himself only with the greatest difficulty? If man is essen-

tially perfect, as the deepest spiritual thinkers maintain, why has this illusion of the "me" been put upon him?

A: Is it Reality that has put man in this situation or is man himself doing it unto himself? Let us rather ask: Why does man bind himself in all sorts of conceptual relationships based on mere acceptance or hearsay, slavish imitation of what others believe, desire, and fear — in sum, through his own unawareness, lack of insight through laziness of a mind that repeats rather than investigates for itself?

Now, the premise that man has to tangle with *Maya* is actually incorrect. It is the mind of man that has brought about *Maya* in the first place and given it continuity through his erroneous identifications and fixations on ideas. And, at the same time, this mind that is asking the original question about man's miserable fate, is it not itself the product of misapprehension, of misuse of consciousness? Has it any right to ask the question, and have its ruminations any validity?

Man is his own enslaver, and therefore his own liberator. And there can be no other liberator! So why blame Reality?

Q: *You have said that "objects" are only appearances and not absolutely real. But since different persons have identical impressions of an object, does this not prove its reality?*

A: It proves only something about impressions, and what does "identical impressions" mean? Who can judge whether your "blue" is the same as my "blue" impression? Or my "sweetness" is like yours? Each observer has his own very individual perception of the world. This is because "perception" depends on the make-up of the percipient — it is not separate from it—and each percipient is the sum-total of his particular conditioning, both psychologically and biologically. Thus, each of us really lives in a world of his own, has his own reality, and the phenomenal world is part of that individual relationship.

Q: Does this not contradict your frequently stated observation that all Reality is One?

A: No, it does not. We cannot mix different levels of meaning. Just now we have been talking about the body-mind entity and its relation to the world. By definition, this is a dualistic relationship, on the level of Manifestation or *Maya*, and essentially represents the "you" and the "me." The reality perceived by these is a *relative* one — a body-mind reality, self-defined by the limited entity. Oneness comes into being only with the Unmanifest, with the transcendence of all limitation. Then you are talking about the Absolute — and the Absolute does not admit of levels, It being beyond all duality.

Q: I see this vase on the table very clearly. Someone else comes up with an identical description of the object. Does this not prove that the object really exists and we all perceive the same reality?

A: The description, the word, may well be identical. But, because the label is the same, does this prove that the object underlying it is perceived identically? At one time, early in my life, I perceived this object and someone pointed to it and said: "This is a vase." Henceforth, whenever I come upon a similar object, I state this fact of my observing a vase. My statement does not say how I perceive the vase — how I sense its color, texture, and its exact size and shape.

Q: But if two or more persons draw the vase, they come up with about the same picture of it.

A: In the first place, the graphic illustration of the vase is not the vase, just as the word is not the thing; it is only a symbol of the vase. Second, the rebuttal argument given for the actual vase applies equally to its graphic representation.

Q: If, in a quiet moment, I look into myself, I see no entity, just nothingness. But, to use an analogy, since the eye cannot see itself, does this observation actually prove there is no ego?

A: Indeed, the eye that sees cannot see itself. But when the mind is very still and I look within, I see that I am absolutely nothing, and at the same time there is the perception that nothingness is everything, the very plenitude of life. We need not go any further than that, because the direct seeing into the Void has completely stilled all questioning of a restless mind. To see one's own total unimportance voids any argument about the existence of an ego. In the very perception of one's voidness one sees how thought has been pursuing the illusory self-importance and that it is this very striving to keep illusion afloat that is the dynamic equivalent of what we call "ego."

In sum, we are faced with a curious situation. The body has no identity of its own, and only the mind can give it identity — but the latter is not legally entitled to do so, for it is nothing in itself! Thus, neither body nor mind has identity and now one sees that not only on the psychological level but also on the physical level there is no separation between the individual "selves"!

Does one see the implications of the latter statement? It means that space-time has contracted into a dimensionless point! And what we have been doing is exactly the opposite process of what Maharaj calls the objectivization of the self. We have thrown new light on the concept of "identity" and shown that the latter is indeed a hypothetical concept, since identity has no meaning in the context of the Universe — nothing has self-nature. All and everything is the Self!

Q: Will the world disappear after my body has disappeared? Where will I be after the body has gone?

A: Space-time, and thereby the world, comes with the body. One can only project into the future while one has this body. Without the body, there is no world to appear or disappear. In the deep sleep state, when the body is quiescent, where is the world? It is obvious that both body-consciousness and world-consciousness appear and disappear at the same time — that is, apart from the body there is no world at all. Now it may be argued that while I am asleep, others are awake and observe the world; this continuous world-appearance to other witnesses proves that there is a world which has independent existence. But Sri Ramana Maharshi pointed out that this argument is fallacious, since the "witnesses" are themselves part of the world whose reality is in question. Therefore, their statements represent inadmissible evidence! They could only be considered valid, if there were some independent evidence for the reality of the witnesses. Since none is forthcoming, the argument is really a subtle form of begging the question, or a circular argument.

"Where will I be after the body has gone?" At the same place where you are now and have always been. Your question will be adequately answered only when you fully understand what the "I" is now, at this very moment, while having this body.

Q: When talking about the three states of existence — waking, dreamless sleep, and dreaming — you appear to equate the dream state with the waking state as to its reality content. I feel the waking state is the only reality.

A: Why do we regard the waking state as a deeper reality than the dream state? Two facts should alert us as to the relativity of both states:

(1) There is interpenetration of both states. On waking up from a dream that has affected us strongly, there is not

an immediate total return of the waking reality. There is, as it were, superimposition of the dream images onto the waking-state "realities." We say, the dream still haunts us. Or for quite some time we experience either satisfaction or unfulfillment with respect to the outcome of the dream. And, conversely, our waking-state reality frequently colors or finds continuity in our dream fantasies.

(2) If the ratio of waking time to sleep time were reversed, would we still feel that the waking reality is the norm and thus represents the real? The truth, of course, is that both the dream "reality" and the waking "reality" are relativities — they are relative to the experiencing mind. When it is perceived that ultimately the mind itself is not, the world perceived in our waking state is seen to be as unreal as the dream world.

Now people argue that there is a difference not only in content but also experientially between the states. That is, the waking state has more of the feel of reality to it than the dream state, and so, intuitively, we feel, is the real. But *when* do people say so? In the waking state, not while dreaming. And while it is true that the waking experience seems more real than the dream experience, that is so only through comparison with the memory of the dream state. During the latter, the experience feels every bit as real as the waking experience during the waking state. Thus, the objection is negated by the symmetry of the situation.

Ultimately, the truth dawns upon us that the waking and dream states are equivalent in that they are both unreal, and that the real must be that which underlies both of these states as well as the deep sleep state. Its full realization leads to the dissolution of the fear of living, which generally manifests itself as a fundamental anxiety or angst. Everyone knows the relief experienced upon waking from a particularly bad dream, which is due to the seeing that our fears are not real; they were only part of the dream. The relief is now extended to the fears of our waking experience. They are seen to be no less of a dream and this brings its own relief — the insight that what we are in our selves — i.e., the Real — can in no way be affected. First, that self embraces everything, and so there are no external factors to affect it. And, second, being itself beyond space-time, it is what is in eternity; this means that there are no grounds for one's fear of death either.

Q: What is the meaning of the "Emptiness" you talk about?

A: Our first step in approaching the Emptiness which is beyond conceptualization is obviously and naturally to think of our ordinary concept of emptiness, which is based upon a physical connotation, and, by implication, its opposite term, fullness. Now, one may get a *feeling* of the Emptiness upon dismissing from one's thinking all traces of these concepts of "emptiness" and "fullness"! Thereby one dismisses totally the entire space-time world structure in the physical sense. Then proceed in the same way in the psychological sense! To dismiss thus-ly (quite simply) *all* concepts from the mind, to go beyond thinking itself, brings into being an extraordinary silence which may become the gateway to the Void which is conceptless.

What we have described so laboriously in the above manner is seen to involve the very voiding of the Emptiness initially arrived at. On the other hand, the true Void, if experienced spontaneously and immediately, does not need being voided — it is itself beyond voiding!

Q: How can I function in that Void in an appropriate manner and yet without a sense of purpose?

A: Currently, you are looking at it from the limited point of view in which all activity is goal-oriented, since we live wholly in and for time. It is like trying to measure Infinity with a yardstick. To begin to understand the question, one needs an entirely different perspective. First fully live in that Void, then your question will automatically be resolved for you and all will be clear.

Q: Does not the Emptiness, to be truly called that, need a container, just like space, consciously or unconsciously, is predicated upon a container of that space?

A: No, this is where the analogy with the concept of physical emptiness breaks down. The Emptiness, unlike physical emptiness, is all that is. It is primordial, and therefore is not held by a container but itself holds the container, or one might say, it is its own container. Everything subsists by virtue of that Emptiness; therefore, it may also be called the Fullness or Plenitude.

Q: When you state that life has meaning but no purpose, what do you mean by "meaning" and what is the difference between "meaning" and "purpose"?

A: "Purpose" demands action, effort, fulfillment, and therefore time to achieve that purpose. It signifies that the present has no actual meaning because all the time I am working towards that purpose, which lies in the future. So my existence has no significance in itself, since it is a mere means to an end. Naturally, we are not talking here about my variegated utilitarian activities, which are rightly goal-oriented, but are discussing the urge for personal fulfillment through purposeful activity, to accomplish some psychological end. So long as I am doing this, that which matters to me lies beyond living, life in the present, and I am effectively writing off that life; my goal lies beyond it, in a so-called purpose — a "what will be," which I value more highly than what *is*. So I am ever wedded to a process of "becoming," never to simply being.

Now "meaning" is quite different in that it is immediate; it does not make any demands. I wholeheartedly embrace existence *as it is*. There is a fulfillment here and now, and therefore it is a timeless state. Life has tremendous meaning for those who can see and hear and feel, who are sensitive enough to all its nuances. Meaning implies contentment and peace, since I lack nothing, am complete as I am. I do not need to make any movement towards a goal that is removed from the here and now by space and time. I realize that I am already liberated, have always been, because, in essence, there are no restraints on my freedom but my own thoughts. As I have accepted myself completely the way I am, there is absolutely no movement to go anywhere, psychologically speaking. I find myself in a state of creative silence or Emptiness from which all things spring eternally and through which all things renew themselves from moment to moment. It means being at one with the Source.

Q: Krishnamurti in one of his Talks rejects the ancient concept of the "witness." What really is the witness, or is he imaginary?

A: What is the process of "choiceless awareness," if it is not that of the witness? Being choicelessly aware is silently witnessing oneself. However, not only is the witnessing a process but also the witness itself is a process in which no center of witnessing is involved. Thus, the witness as another entity that consciousness can identify with must be rejected; but as an actual process it can open the door to enlightenment in a very potent way.

Q: What happens to the person after death?

A: Nothing happens but the disintegration of the body. Why should anything fundamental happen on physical death? As far as Reality is concerned, it is a superficial event. Consciousness is not affected, because consciousness does not dwell in the body, or exist for the body, but the body dwells in consciousness — it is a creation of the latter.

Q: What is the difference between consciousness and awareness, which difference is apparently maintained by Sri Nisargadatta?

A: Consciousness has content; awareness is that which makes the consciousness possible. It is like the perception of light, which makes objects visible — analogously to consciousness. But the discernment between light and dark is analogous to awareness.

Q: Why do we always seem to slip backward in self-inquiry?

A: The problem can perhaps be usefully restated as follows: Why does the mind ever reassert itself and fall back into its old habits, even after, in a moment of creative silence, its pernicious nature (from the point of view of psychological freedom) has been perceived?

It appears to me that a number of factors are at work. First in importance is the pleasure-pain principle, the mind's drive to seek and assure itself pleasure and avoid pain — which is its "emotional security." Man, once he has tasted pleasure, cannot let go of it. It is as simple as that. So the brain continues to faithfully register every experience relevant to the pleasure-pain principle. It is even doubtful whether there would be a mind at all without this center that cultivates pleasure for its own sake through desire and gratification. Similarly, it is doubtful whether desire actually exists in its own right, independent of this center, since fundamentally and paradoxically, the mind — through a four-stage process of imagination, projection, cultivation, and self-sensitization — creates its own desire. Seeing, therefore, that its mainspring is pleasure, how can the mind voluntarily abstain without destroying itself? It goes against everything it stands for.

Then, there is this thing called "habit." Habit in bodily function is, as we all know, difficult to eradicate — look at the smoker, the drinker, the excessive eater, and so forth. Just so with the mind, which is only another aspect of the body-mind entity. Now, who is in control? Is it not the mind, and so the habit itself? Those of us who have occasionally been bewitched by some "haunting" melody will know how it continues to repeat itself by its own momentum, even though we are heartily sick of it and dearly wish for some peace and quiet. So it goes not only with "overwhelming" ideations, obsessions, but also the entire collection of "inclinations," tendencies of the mind, unresolved conflicts, hang-ups, desires, anxieties, expectations, etc. In fact, according to Buddhism, this bundle of mind elements, termed "skandhas," constitutes the very ego. And to expect the mind or ego to deal harshly and, therefore, honestly with the ego is, in Ramana Maharshi's words, like the thief turned policeman trying to catch the thief, which is himself.

So is there no help at all? Are we doomed forever to persist in our unhappy ways? The logic of the foregoing brings forth its own answer. If the mind — which is essentially memory and its re-activation, and so continuity in time — is the problem, then I must open myself to that which has no continuity, that which is from moment to moment, a new dimension, as it were, that of the timeless.

Let us remember, only thought has continuity; existence has no continuity except through thought, which is time. So by the very fact of standing back from my thought, merely observing and not in any way participating. I have disengaged myself from continuity. Thought and awareness are mutually exclusive. When I am fully attentive, the past has no more significance. Having liberated the moment, I no longer look back. And I am free to be out of it, entirely, out of all the travail of daily existence, which comes into being only with the continuity of the "me," which is the encapsulated past. No longer being identified with that artificial entity, the creation of memory, let fate's arrows hit where they may: in a sense, I have made myself invisible and so invulnerable. Remaining ever vigilant, ever watchful, I stand away in ecstasy (literally, "beside myself"). Subjectively, there is the distinct feeling of unreality where it concerns "myself." Things that happen to this body feel like they are happening to a person other than "myself," and things happening to others are in some way also affecting this body. And even if I lose that attentiveness, the liberating awareness, I know for certain that I have it within my capability to snap back into it at any moment, merely by being quiet and silently observing the process of my own thoughts.

Q: *Do you believe in the reality of "miracles"?*

A: I neither believe nor disbelieve in "miracles." Nor do I approach this question with any sense of religious meaningfulness. Most religious people see miracles as some kind of certification of their religious leader, a divine sign that their man is on to something significant.

Knowing that the infinite power behind the world process, or the infinite Potentiality, is neither matter nor mind, but underlies both, means that one must keep open the possibility of miracles but it does not prove their actual existence. To me, what are conventionally called "miracles" are of no special importance, except possibly as a scientific curiosity, seeing that really everything manifest is a miracle of creation! What greater miracle can there be than the creation of the myriads of creatures and "things" from the Void that is "No-thingness" or Infinite Potentiality?

41 ❧

Probings

The mind itself is a mere psychological reflex mechanism. Without awareness, it is nothing and cannot function, just as a fire without fuel is not a fire. It is awareness that gives us life, intelligence; without it, we would be no more than a lump of coal.

※

Either one examines the outer and so comes to an understanding of the inner, or one examines the inner and so comes to an understanding of the outer. The latter is the preferred way, but in either case one arrives at the insight of the essential identity of the outer and the inner.

※

Paradoxically, we do not come to self-knowledge, which is essentially knowing that which is non-self, because we are too much captivated by what we are *not*, the ego. Yet, this is the way to self-knowledge: seeing the false as the false — the *via negativa* — to travel from unreality to reality.

~~~

The mind must go out of existence. The mind is an instrument of focusing, and only that — it always narrows down and fragments that which is *whole*, that which *is*. Like a lens that focuses the light falling upon it, so the mind concentrates the field of attention, focuses it, and in the process causes distortion. Whatever is touched by the mind suffers from this distortion which is corruption.

So one has to learn to observe without the interference of the mind, when one's vision will be kept pure, whole.

~~~

A meaningful life is not a purposeful life. On the contrary, in order to discover the meaningful, one has to die to all that which is merely purposeful, which includes even the intellectual search for the meaningful. A life filled exclusively with purposeful activity is a tragic mistake. And there is meaning only for the individual, for society ever pushes the individual toward end-related endeavors, which leads to a mechanical, fragmentary existence. One has to take a stand against such pressures, which requires an understanding of the process and infinite alertness.

Meaningfulness knows no content, for content is important only so long as the split between subject and object has not been healed. Meaningfulness signifies to be carried by a powerful current of energy; or rather, one is that energy which is beginningless and endless, yet renews itself at every moment.

⟋

When all is said and done, what can be done? Only one thing: to stop daydreaming — to be so aware of every desire and moment of fear that one wakes up into that state in which fear and desire are not any more than pinpoints in the fabric of time.

⟋

We all have "assumed" identities!

⟋

As far as the possibility of self-realization is concerned, there is really only one problem: to deflate (completely) our feeling of self-importance. Self-importance is the seed crystal around which the entire unreal world of duality accretes.

But what ground have we for self-importance? Our physical self has a totally uncertain existence: at any moment it faces an ending, which therefore also applies to the psychological self or "mind." Even the tiniest microbe competes on even terms with our physical self for survival. In reality, what we are bodily is totally insignificant. From nature's point of view, our continuity, except as a species — which is not pertinent to the individual — has an extremely low order of priority.

In the state of mere external freedom, there is a certain joyful feeling in the anticipation of all the things that one is going to do with that freedom. When one is actually doing those things so eagerly anticipated, one may find them not so attractive after all. In the state of internal freedom, there is a joy purely and simply for being part of life, for being what one is — without any dependencies on external factors, whatever one's physical situation may be and whatever "roles" one has assumed in society.

It may be said that we are already the Supreme; so what is the need to do anything? What is the need for self-realization?

Yes, we are the Supreme, but we do not function as we could or should: effortlessly, spontaneously, blissfully. There is ignorance, suffering, all this is part of the Supreme; but so long as we are identified with a fragmentary vision, we are — by choice — mere fragments, and so are likely to be buffeted by every storm that comes our way. Now it might be thought that if, by logical extension, one identifies with the All instead of the fragment of the self, one will automatically function correctly. This would be wrong, however, for an ideation, no matter how lofty, is still only a thought or an image and thereby subject to limitation. Only if one identifies with nothing at all — that is, the absence of *any* kind of identification — will there take place a merger with Nothingness and a regaining of one's natural state. And then there will also be a knowing, which is *being*: to be a totality within oneself, to be *That*.

———

It is true that we are the engine of God, but as long as the ignition is not turned on, it is a non-functioning engine. To ignite one's consciousness is God-realization.

———

Beauty is in the eyes of the beholder, as they say; no, *everything* is in the eyes of the beholder. For the beholder is the beheld, the observer is the observed. And, similarly, the objects of desire are created by the beholder: the conditioned entity that entertains "desires."

———

We should study consciousness more — its nature and its arising; all we are concerned with now is the contents of consciousness.

———

The ordinary, worldly man gets the worst of both worlds. Clinging to his separate existence, which is synonymous with sorrow, he also fears death — the psychological ending which would heal his sorrowful condition.

———

In a striking analogy, the mind that is healthiest is just like the body: it is least noticed! When you are not aware of your body, it functions quietly, efficiently; so also your mind functions as it should when it does not throw up all kinds of psychological problems.

———

It is a pity that the words "spiritual life" were ever invented, for they have caused so much confusion. For, in truth, there is only life — the everyday life — which is simply what is at every moment. And there is nothing wrong with that life, if only thought would leave it alone and not try to make it into something that it is not.

———

"Getting in touch with oneself" is part of one's responsibility for good health and well-being. It means to me basically knowing the tolerance of one's psychosomatic machinery by perceiving one's limitations — physically, intellectually, and in every other way. To know when one has exceeded these limits, by feeling that something is wrong with one's being and then being able to rectify and prevent it through natural biofeedback — all this is based on the fact that, with perfect physical or mental health, one is simply not aware of one's soma or psyche.

———

Self-knowing is only to be approached through knowing what one is not. In one sense of the word, it is not even possible to "get in touch with one's self" — that applies only to the psychosomatic part of one's being — one can only *be* one's self, which happens when the psychosomatic machinery no longer interferes and no longer deceives us by posing as a pseudo-self.

~~~

We ever want to get something *out* of life, and therefore, by implication, separate ourselves from life; for, in truth, we *are* that life.

~~~

We strive to "realize our dreams," as we say — and, in fact, mere dreams they are, relevant only on the dream level, the *Maya* level, of our existence. This striving, therefore, only strengthens the obstacles to liberation.

~~~

What is the need for religion, for a so-called spiritual orientation in life, at all? If living is a natural function, like breathing, then why interfere? Why can we not continue in our naturally more or less hedonistic ways? This would be true if our minds were still functioning in their natural ways, free from complexity, flowing with life. This assumption, as we all know, is no longer true — if it ever has been. Our minds are heavily conditioned, fragmented and deeply in contradiction. This deep conflict in the mind leads inevitably to conflict in society, and thus to chaos. So even if we opted for a simple, hedonistic way of life, sooner or later this would be compromised by the ways of the mind.

True religion or spirituality is nothing other than the reversal of this whole process of chaos, conflict, to a state of simplicity, naturalness, and therefore order. Meditation is the first step — an investigation to find out whether such a reversal to a more natural condition is at all possible, and what is and what is not necessary for bringing it about.

<hr>

The mind does not really exist. What exists are the thoughts only. The substrate of the mind is thought; not: the mind is the substrate of thought. The thought "To whom does this happen?" is the most powerful tool in the quest. It cuts right at the root of our world of unreality. It is the most effective in dissolving sorrow — the sorrow that ensues from the postulation of the false "I."

<hr>

The mind's everlasting tendency to seek stability and order for itself in an insecure and disorderly world seems to me the exact counterpart of a concept in physics called "entropy" — the tendency for physical states to proceed from the more to the less complex, from instability to stability, from heterogeneity to uniformity. One might call this propensity of the mind "spiritual entropy." It reaches a maximum upon the psychological death of the organism, which constitutes its liberation.

＊

Physical Entropy + Spiritual Entropy = Asymmetry of Time. Here, "Asymmetry of Time" stands for time as a one-way arrow.

＊

We talk about pure and impure thought, but how can there be? The so-called innocent — except as infants—may not be worldly wise, but they live in their own dreamworlds. All thought being derived from experience, and so a form of conditioning, "pure" and "impure" lose their meaning. True innocence is only to be found prior to consciousness, in the state of beingness, before the stirring of thought.

＊

From the spiritual point of view the most unhelpful phrases in the English language are "If only," and "What if?," and the most pertinent "So what?" and "Who cares!?" — the latter, especially when uttered from the state of creative emptiness.

＊

You can shed your burdens only when you let go of your identity.

＊

Man, once he has created himself as a separate entity, feels insecure, frightened and lonely, due to the inherent labile state of affairs of being an island of unreality. In this condition, every impression is stored in memory. Impressions are a shield against the Emptiness, which represents Death, or total destruction. So continuity becomes a psychological need and this is the root cause of anchoring oneself in a particular environment, a particular set-up, a particular frame of reference. The frame of reference per se is, of course, meaningless, but my collective memories — the "I" — being in it and of it, have made it meaningful.

The question of whether or not memory needs brain cells, is it not another example of thinking from the body-mind schism? Is it not another chicken-or-egg type of question, on the fundamental level, which cannot therefore have an answer?

There are two alternative modes of functioning for the mind. One, in which thought uses Intelligence for its own purposes, and remains the predominant factor — our ordinary state of being — and the other, in which Intelligence uses thought as a tool and only where appropriate — the state of freedom.

The mind is a totally mechanical thing: so long as it operates it excludes spirituality, the action of Intelligence. Unfortunately, we are totally unaware of this mechanicalness, this limitation, which is so clearly demonstrated by the fact that when we wish to designate mechanical-ness, we call it "mind*less*" activity. We are pretty good at understanding and controlling mechanical devices, but here the difficulty is that this mind *is us*.

⤖

There is a paradox in self-knowing, isn't there? All one can ever know about oneself is what one is *not*. To know all one's characteristics, all one's inclinations, all one's habits is necessarily a negative approach to self-knowing, yet the only one possible. For only when we fully know what we are not can the self shine forth with its own self-luminous radiance.

⤖

In realizing oneself as a mere conduit of experience, and not as an experiencer, lies an extraordinary ecstasy: a sense of freedom from clinging to existence — which is the transcendence of life and death. And how does one avoid becoming an "experiencer"? By not being an *accumulator* of experience. By not in any way clinging to experience, the contents of memory — except on the most impersonal, factual level. When one lets go of every experience — simply letting events happen — and by fully digesting (i.e., understanding) the significance of every experience within one's self-projected frames of reference, there is never any residue left and so one's consciousness is constantly being emptied. Then the mind remains unburdened and vital, fully concentrated in the present.

Real Knowledge is to know that all that binds us is mere knowledge: ideas, concepts, images, all in thought, upon which the "me" — itself only a construct of thought — has built a psychological dependency by means of attachment.

If essentially one is a mere conduit for experiences of all kinds, what happens to bring about the "experiencer"? One way in which our activities on the psychological level may be characterized is that of giving meaning to the essentially meaningless, the mere experience. This builds the personally significant, and, thereby, the "personal" — that is, giving rise to the "persona" and "self-importance." In this light we may see the significance given to, for example, anniversaries, ceremonies; the always looking back, as "nostalgia," thereby further imprinting memory of past events in the brain. All this brings into being a continuity for a series of events, images, selected experiences, that in their totality we cherish as the "me" and which becomes the central but hidden motivating force in our life. But using the term "selected experiences," it may be asked: Is not there, intrinsically, a selector and so an *a priori* "me"? No, it happens through the mechanism of psychological memory itself: the pleasurable experiences, as well as the painful ones, with the most emotional impact, are retained — either consciously or unconsciously; the others drop away into oblivion.

⊸⊶

You do have control over your affairs, your life — to the extent that fate allows . . . .

⊸⊶

Supposing there were some kind of clock-like mechanism in the brain, but instead of measuring time it would actually "make" time, so that man would be able to "measure" it. (It is a trick the mechanism performs by utilizing a tape recorder type of device in which cells have the capacity to play back an impression, giving rise to "memory.") A bit of a farce, wouldn't it be, if taken seriously!? But that is exactly the condition that prevails in reality. And, believe it or not, we do take it seriously so that our every move in life depends on psychological time — the idea that we must ever get "better." Thus, we are completely dominated by this fictitious tyrant in an eternal process of "becoming"!

⊸⊶

In everyday life we are told not to look at issues in a black-and-white manner, but to consider all the intermediate shades of gray. In the spiritual life, and more generally, whenever we are considering fundamental issues, the converse applies. Things are either so, or they are not; there is no question of "yes, but . . ." Analogously to the either/or principle that predominates scientific evidence of the behavior of natural phenomena (witness, e.g., the basis of the quantum theory), so all fundamental issues, when clearly seen, are ever sharply delineated.

⸺⸙⸺

I feel like an outsider being set down for a sojourn upon this earth, where I do not have any vested interests and am therefore a mere observer. Having had no say in the matter of my emergence — "I" (as a body-mind entity) consider myself strictly as a temporary appearance/disappearance phenomenon — I am not rooted in space-time. This implies a certain playfulness on my part, because it is in the nature of my being and particular destiny that I cannot take anything with absolute seriousness, since I do not live with absolutes. There is nothing to lose for me nor to gain. Hence, I cannot do many things without a strong sense of adventurousness, or fun, for my ulterior motives (if one can call them that) for any action are curiosity (in the sense of an urge for inquiry) and playfulness.

⸺⸙⸺

When I begin to be aware of my real being, I see that I am not one of an infinite multiplicity, but I am the commonality, the background, upon which the multiplicity has been falsely projected. The painful aspect of the initial realization lies in the fact that I must drop completely out of the comparative scene which is inherent in multiplicity, which leads to a structure of hierarchy in any human society and from which is derived most of our thinking and acting. What all this implies is that I must give up my being as an "individual" which I had cherished and cultivated so unthinkingly throughout a lifetime.

The other day I read a survey in a local newspaper, in which a number of people were questioned as to what was the thing in their life for which they were most thankful. One lady stated she was most thankful for the mere fact of being alive, and how it was so much better than not having been born at all.

I could not help being intrigued by her answer and began to contemplate the observation on a deeper level than was probably intended, or imagined, by the interviewee. Does the remark have any real meaning? For, in reality, she always is her Self, eternally; she is her Self regardless of birth and also of death, for both the latter apply only to the body.

Put in a different way, one could ask: Since she compares her situation with the state of not having been born at all, then who is unborn and what is the condition of not having been born?

Meditating on this, one comes to the conclusion that the question was based on the wrong premise and therefore meaningless. All is the Self, timelessly, although bodies may come and go, and one is — and can never be anything but — the Eternal Consciousness, the Absolute. The condition of "not having been born at all" is a mere mental projection, devoid of reality. There never is an alternative for her to being her Self.

<hr />

Even if the mind were to come up with some evidence it was an absolute, independent entity, validating the existence of a separate individuality or "ego," what would such proof be worth? Nothing! The proof would be valid only to the entity whose absolute existence is in doubt in the first place. A perfectly circular argument, indeed!

<hr />

Man (i.e., the mind) perceives an inside and an outside — in other words, space-time — but, in truth, both that outside and inside are emanations of his "I am" consciousness, projections by the mind so that it may objectify itself (body-mind) and other things, the totality of which comprises the world. When one realizes the source of this limited consciousness, one knows that the "inside" and "outside" are part of something else, which transcends space-time. Therefore, one stands apart from the body — both one's own and others' — and realizes that the whole world is the creation of that source-consciousness.

How could I hang on to an "individuality" and thereby maintain the fear of death, once I have clearly seen that all "I" am is a bundle of memories which of their own accord seek to gather further memories (experiences)? (That is, there is no coordinator of these memories except the memories themselves!) Memories seek out further memories, like iron filings are drawn and cling to a magnet — a purely mechanical process

It is not only the psychological images that we hold of ourselves, but also the body images that influence our behavior. So it is that in every step of our development, the genetically determined body molds the mind, the many roles we perform as male, female, teenager, middle-aged person, etc. In this respect, we faithfully fulfill the expectations of the various society-imposed stereotypes.

Just as nature has arranged it so that one cannot stay asleep (dreaming) and be aware that one is asleep (dreaming) at the same time — one wakes up immediately — so within this so-called waking state one cannot remain as one is — unawakened — upon realizing that one is actually living in a dream state.

It is interesting to note that to be free of time or dwell in the timeless state, one should paradoxically view oneself and one's actions from the perspective of a frame of reference that contains the totality of one's chronological life span. This means there is no fixation upon a particular point in time, and therefore no possibility of identification with a pseudo-entity that could be construed as a "person."

In such a context, time stands for "body," and the dispassionate overview signifies the freeing from the identification with body and the attachments produced by the clinging to certain memory images.

—⊙—

The spiritual nature of man becomes meaningful only upon the discovery of the changeless substratum of the changeful. Man in his present condition is so alienated from this timeless reality, his real nature, that he thinks the changeful is the norm. Being ensconced in a shell of the changeful, which is the passing show of life's drama, he has accepted this firmly as the Ultimate. And when someone confronts him with a different state of consciousness, that of the Changeless, he demands proof of its existence! But is not this a logical impossibility for the temporal, the transient, to fathom the immensity of the Changeless? For by necessity, the temporal perceiver must immediately transform all that is into data of a temporal kind, as otherwise it would be beyond his grasp. This also means that there is nothing this perceiver, as a temporal entity, can actively do to embrace the timeless consciousness. He can only go from the incomplete, the fragmented, to the incomplete, the fragmented, remaining ever within the sphere of the limited and never reaching the Totality. In this connection, to make us aware of our plight, Sri Nisargadatta Maharaj keeps asking the question: Who are you and where are you proceeding to? Thus, he points to the need for self-inquiry, for most of us do not know who we are, not realizing the fact that we are on an everlasting treadmill to nowhere. The question of our identity and our involvement in, and attachment to, the changeful are fully interdependent. If one truly understands what and how "I am," the attachment to the changeful is at once fallen away, and, conversely, understanding how we are held in a conceptual network gives immediate insight into what one is and exposes the mythical "individuality." Then it becomes clear that the question is not whether apart from the constantly changing there also exists that which could be called the Changeless. For just as the snake-like appearance of a rope is correctly identified as nothing but rope, so the changeful is finally seen for what it is: unreal, appearance only, a projection onto that which can only be the Changeless.

What is this thing that considers itself the doer and ever seeks its own continuity? Once the real nature of this "I" is correctly understood and seen to be nothing more than a collection of memories (experiences) gathering further memories by seeking new experiences, then why should one cling to life? For that "clinging to life" would mean only to maintain such an unsubstantial entity in such a meaningless pursuit.

Not only are things not what they seem to be, but whatever is observed and thought about cannot be the real; for any observation and any thinking necessarily entails a subject-object duality and can therefore only refer to fragments — never the Whole.

The real is that which lies between the subject and the object but does not recognize either.

Things and thoughts — are they ever real? Yes and no. They are real for the body-mind only, but the latter is itself a limitation on what is Real. Since beyond that — in the Absolute sense — body-mind cannot be considered real, any observation made by or through that entity is of the same quality; that is, it cannot be real, or rather the discussion whether it is real or unreal is meaningless, being merely a play within the field of Ignorance.

Advaita reigns in the Beingness and only there; beyond that — in the Absolute — the question of *advaita* or *dvaita* becomes meaningless.

Can one imagine a greater Magician than the one

who has created the Supreme Illusion of Maya? Each living creature with the capacity of self-awareness regards the world as being external to itself rather than internal and self-created, and therefore considers itself as being within the world, within a matrix of space-time. And each human being looks upon the testimony of others as validation for his own erroneous "world" view, for he does not realize that this very same delusion equally obtains in all other "individuals" whereby each erects his own "world" around his body image.

We can now see that this chain of delusion — a veritable mass deception — could well go on forever, if it were not for a happy encounter with the sat-guru, who teaches that truth lies in the exact opposite direction. For the benefit of our awakening, he points out that in reality there is only one Self, which is prior to space and time, and therefore indivisible and Eternal. Like the all-pervading space, which makes possible the appearance of all things and beings, this Self is the source of all and everything but remains in itself ungraspable and ineffable.

Inspiring Books from Blue Dove Press

Discovering the Realm Beyond Appearance
Pointers to the Inexpressible
by Robert Powell, Ph.D
Softcover   200 pp. $14.00   ISBN: 1-884997-17-1

"Dr. Powell is one of the best known Western writers on Advaita *philosophy.... All those seeking higher levels of awareness will find powerful tools in* Discovering the Realm Beyond Appearance.*"*— **Deepak Chopra**
Author of *The Seven Spiritual Laws of Success*

Excerpt from the book:
"The meaning of your existence is primarily to realize your true nature, that you are not just an 'individual,' so that your life may stand in service of the world as a whole and make it a little less miserable. All else is mere entertainment, without ultimate meaning....

"But once you have realized your true nature, when individuality has been seen for the illusion it is and so has been transcended once and for all, there is only the Totality. Now where could the Totality go? It is at once everything, completely fulfilled—it is fulfillment itself. Therefore, the question of meaning cannot apply for one, or more accurately, for That which has realized itself. We can only talk of 'meaning' when there is intentionality, direction, a movement from here to there, from incomplete to complete, applying to a fragment, the false image of an 'entity.' It could not possibly apply to that which by definition is Everything, Complete and Perfect in Itself."
                              —**Robert Powell**

Dialogues on Reality

An Exploration into the Nature of Our Ultimate Identity
by Robert Powell, Ph.D.
Softcover   236 pp. $14   ISBN: 1-884997-16-3

"Dr. Powell is one of the best known Western writers on
Advaita *philosophy. He comments elegantly on the insights of*
Krishnamurti and Sri Nisargadatta Maharaj, and explains his
own insights on the nature of the unified state. You will find
great gems in his books. "— **Deepak Chopra**
Author of *Ageless Body, Timeless Mind* and *Quantum*
Healing

Dr. Powell is widely recognized as one of the most
inspired writers on the subject of *Advaita*, the teaching of non-
duality. He takes us on a journey beyond the realm of the ego,
beyond the subject and object, good and bad, high and low, to
the ground on which the manifest universe rests. This is where
the mind and intellect cannot reach and which is beyond words.
Yet in this book, Dr. Powell does a masterful job clearly
indicating the path to where we have ever been.

Excerpt from the book:
"You see, the psychologist starts from the wrong basis. His
methodology is founded upon the assumption that there really
is a 'person,' an ego, that can be free, whereas what we are
trying to point out is that the ego itself, which comprises both
the conscious and the unconscious, is totally a composite of
falseness and the source of all trouble; it alone destroys
freedom and nothing else does...You see that you are not within
the world, you are not a small entity in a very large world but
the opposite is the case...The whole world of phenomena,
entities, creatures, is within my consciousness. And that
consciousness has no boundaries, no divisions; it is infinity
itself. " — **Robert Powell**

The Ultimate Medicine
As Prescribed by Sri Nisargadatta Maharaj
Edited by Robert Powell, Ph.D.
Softcover   240 pp. $14   ISBN: 1-884997-09-0

"...Nisargadatta, like all the great sages of old India, elucidates the nature of the Ultimate Reality clearly and simply. He makes the highest Self-realization a matter of common understanding so that any sincere seeker can grasp the essence of it."
— **David Frawley, O.M.D.**, author of *Beyond the Mind,* and *Ayurvedic Healing*

"...Sri Nisargadatta Maharaj will be increasingly recognized as a wholly admirable star in the spiritual firmament of our age."
— **Peter V. Madill, M.D.**

Sri Nisargadatta Maharaj (1897-1981), one of the most important spiritual preceptors of the twentieth century, lived and taught in a small apartment in the slums of Bombay, India. A realized master of the Tantric Nath lineage, Maharaj had a wife and four children. For many years he supported his family by selling inexpensive goods in a small booth on the streets outside his tenement. His life was a telling parable of the absolute nonduality of Being.

The simple words of this extraordinary teacher are designed to jolt us into awareness of our original nature. His style is abrupt, provocative and immensely profound— wasting little time with nonessentials and cutting directly to the core.

A steady stream of Indians and Westerners came to sit at the feet of Maharaj in the small loft where he received visitors. There, in the tradition of Ramana Maharshi, he shared the highest Truth of nonduality in his own unique way, from the depths of his own realization.

In *The Ultimate Medicine*, Nisargadatta provides advanced instructions for serious spiritual aspirants.

The Nectar of Immortality
Sri Nisargadatta Maharaj's Discourses on the Eternal
Edited by Robert Powell, Ph.D.
Softcover 208 pp. $14 ISBN: 1-884997-13-9

"Nisargadatta Maharaj is my greatest teacher. His words guide my writing, speaking and all of my relationships. The singular pursuit of the awakened person is to find that part of himself or herself that cannot be destroyed by death. I know of no one who can aid you more on that journey than Nisargadatta Maharaj. His wisdom guided me throughout the writing of Your Sacred Self. Let him be with you, as he is always with me, via this profound book, The Nectar of Immortality."
— **Dr. Wayne Dyer**, author of *Your Erroneous Zones* and *Your Sacred Self*

Sri Nisargadatta Maharaj (1897-1981), a revered master of the Tantric Nath lineage, is an inspiring example of an ordinary family man who attained complete realization of the Infinite. Living the absolute nonduality of Being in every moment, he taught that true freedom is a possibility open to every one of us. He drew disciples from all over the world to his humble loft in the tenements of Bombay.

Even on the written page, his words carry a special potency, subtly pushing us beyond the ego to our original, pristine and blissful Self, to the rediscovery of Oneness and authentic liberation in our Source.

"There are no conditions to fulfill. There is nothing to be done, nothing to be given up.... It is your idea that you have to do things that entangle you in the results of your efforts. The motive, the desire, the failure to achieve, the sense of frustration — all this holds you back. Simply look at whatever happens and know that you are beyond it."— **Sri Nisargadatta Maharaj**

The Experience of Nothingness
Sri Nisargadatta Maharaj's Talks on Realizing the Infinite
Edited by Robert Powell, Ph.D.
Softcover   166 pp. $14   ISBN: 1-884997-14-7

"Sri Nisargadatta Maharaj hardly needs an introduction any longer to lovers of the highest wisdom. Known as a maverick Hindu sage, Nisargadatta is now generally acknowledged to rank with the great masters of advaita *teachings, such as Sri Ramana Maharshi...,Sri Atmananda...,and the more recently known disciple of the Maharshi, Poonjaji..."*— **Robert Powell**

In this final volume of the Nisargadatta Maharaj trilogy published by Blue Dove Press, the ever-trenchant Nisargadatta uses Socratic dialogue, wry humor, and his incisive intellect to cut through the play of consciousness which constitutes illusion: this is his only goal. He can relentlessly pursue a logical argument to its very end clearly demonstrating that logic and spirituality do not necessarily stand in opposition to one another.

Nisargadatta uses every device in his command to great effect, turning his visitors' questions back on themselves, making them laugh at the very concept of "concepts" and ultimately revealing that the emperor "mind" indeed has no clothes.

Excerpt from the book:
"Everything that is there, it is fullness and it is nothingness. So long as I do not have that 'I-am-ness,'I no longer have the concept that I am an individual. Then my individuality has merged into this everythingness or nothingness and everything is all right."— **Sri Nisargadatta Maharaj**

Never to Return
A Modern Quest for Eternal Truth
by Sharon Janis

Softcover   330pp. $16.95   ISBN: 1-884997-29-5

"...In a larger sense, this memoir is a dialogue between Indian spirituality and Western psychology. The question that Janis answers in her memoir is: 'Can a westerner come to know Indian spirituality and flourish in its depths, even when it is alien to western ways of knowing?' She answers with a resounding 'Yes.'" — **Publishers Weekly**

This highly acclaimed memoir is both a real-life spiritual adventure and a rare and intimate glimpse into a modern-day search for eternal truth.

Raised an atheist, author Sharon Janis survived a painful and dysfunctional childhood with a strength, independence, and curiosity that awakened in her a voracious spiritual hunger. Eventually, her search would take her to an Indian monastery, where she stayed for ten years.

Janis has a natural gift for story-telling and a unique ability to share spiritual insights in an entertaining, easily accessible and novel-like style. Her engagingly humorous and touching personal anecdotes address some of the most delicate topics of human existence: the power and vulnerability of the mind, devotion, death, humility, justice, grace and an infinite freedom beyond outer appearances.

This account also offers an exceptional view into the inner workings of the personal relationship between teacher and student, guru and disciple, an ultimately, the intimacy between the individual and his or her God.

Collision with the Infinite
A Life Beyond the Personal Self
by Suzanne Segal

Softcover   170pp. $14.00   ISBN: 1-884997-27-9

"...Segal describes the profound spiritual experience of the egoless state...Many have tried to do what Segal does, but none have achieved such clarity in the task."—**Publishers Weekly**

"This is an extraordinary account of the experience of selflessness..."—**Joseph Goldstein**, author of *The Experience of Insight*

"...an amazingly honest, fascinating, and vivid account of one woman's awakening to her essential emptiness—and her eventual discovery, through much pain and fear, that as emptiness-fullness it is freedom *from pain and fear...this awakening is available, right now and just as one is, to all who dare to look in at the infinite..."*—**Douglas Harding**, author of *On Having No Head*

"...To anyone interested in the subject, I would say, 'Read this book!'"—**Ramesh S. Balsekar**, author of *Consciousness Speaks*

One day, in the early 1980's, a young American woman, Suzanne Segal, stepped onto a bus in Paris. Suddenly and unexpectedly, she found herself egoless, stripped of any sense of personal self. Struggling for years to make sense of her mental state, she consulted therapist after therapist. Eventually, she turned to spiritual teachers, coming at last to understand that this was the egoless state, that elusive consciousness to which so many aspire— the Holy Grail of so many spiritual traditions.

Written in a spare, unpretentious style, this book is Suzanne Segal's own account of what such a terrifying event meant to her when it crashed into her everyday life.

Mother of All

A Revelation of the Motherhood of God in the Life and Teachings of the Jillellamudi Mother
by Richard Schiffman
Softcover   275 pp. $15.95   ISBN: 1-884997-28-7

When circumstances brought National Public Radio commentator, Richard Schiffman to Jillellamudi in South India, he found himself in the presence of a powerful and compelling woman known as Amma, the Jillellamudi Mother. In this personal and moving account, Schiffman tells us of his several years at the "House of All," Amma's spiritual center, where every visitor was fed and made welcome. Amma was considered by many of those around her, including the author, to be an avatar, an incarnation of the Divine Mother herself. Neither a preacher nor a proselytizer, she taught through her quiet, compassionate presence, encouraging all who remained a while with her to step out of time into the gradual, peaceful understanding of a deliberate and conscious way of living.

Excerpt from the Introduction:

"In Jillellamudi village, South India, there lived a Mother. She fed her children, nursed them in illness, scolded them, cajoled them, comforted their distress, and dried their tears...She was very much like the other mothers, quite ordinary, really, in appearance and manner, with no quirks of character to set her apart. If it were not for one distinctive quality, she would hardly have been noticed, much less worshiped as she is today by untold thousands. What is it that distinguished this Mother from the others? Simply this—whereas usually we limit our affection and consider some few biological progeny alone to be our children, the Mother at Jillellamudi felt that all were her children—all men, all animals, all objects, all thoughts, feelings, qualities—everything, everywhere, she treated with the tender cherishing that mothers lavish on their own. In the whole universe, this Mother found nothing inert, nothing lifeless. And in all the vast multiplicity of life, she saw only her children, appearing endlessly with myriad names, conditions, and forms."

The Play of God

Visions of the Life of Krishna
by Devi Vanamali

Softcover   416 pp. $19.95   ISBN: 1-884997-07-4

"Krishna's biography is an exceptional introduction to the Indian worldview. This is going to become a classic text which opens many doors —doors historical, cultural and spiritual."
— **Publishers Weekly**

"Highly recommended as a fresh and readable presentation, in English, of the life and meaning of Krishna."
— **Library Journal**

"This is a valuable treasure to be cherished."
— **Swami Chidananda**, President of the Divine Life Society, Rishikesh

    The Play of God is the account of a spiritual phenomenon. It describes the extraordinary manifestation of the Eternal in the realm of time that occurred in Krishna, the playful and enchantingly beautiful Deity who embodies the highest truths of India's spiritual vision.   Readers will find here powerful visions of God as child, playmate, friend, and teacher. What is evoked here is not a religion of moral law and stern obligation, but a spirituality of joy and true desire, love and beauty, contemplation and inner awakening.

    Never before has the complete life of Krishna been told in a way that is so engaging and understandable, yet so faithful to the ancient epics of India. The life of Krishna stretches our conception of Divinity and lifts our minds to a higher spiritual plane as we contemplate the unlimited joy of the Eternal appearing to us in a form combining beauty, strength, and astounding playfulness.   Spiritual seekers of all traditions will find faith in these pages.

Treasury of Spiritual Wisdom
Compiled by Andy Zubko
Softcover   528 pp. $19.95   ISBN: 1-884997-10-4

"...a compendium of over 10,000 sagely chosen short sayings by an 'eclectic array of spiritual teachers and thinkers. Organized under 142 alphabetical headings like 'Choice,' 'Growth,' 'Death,' etc., these pithy bits make good reading."
— **Publishers Weekly**

"This 'Bartlett's Quotations for the Soul' is a massive collection of inspirational quotations from sources as diverse as Joan Rivers, Jesus, and the Upanishads, covering topics ranging from abundance and desire to self-esteem and work. Because it will be appropriate for use by students, teachers, and speakers, this handy reference will be a strong addition to all collections. Recommended."— **Library Journal**

Have you ever been baffled by an intractable challenge that seemed to defy solution? Are you the type of person who savors inspiring words? If you are a thoughtful, spiritually conscious person who would like to apply the wisdom of the ages in a practical way to the problems in your life, this handy reference volume will become an indispensable companion.

In this book you'll find the inspiring words of saints, the vision of shamans, the insights of the enlightened, the teachings of prophets, as well as the cutting insights of both the well-known and not-so-well-known from both East and West.

Organized into 142 categories such as Love, Power, Self-Esteem, Adversity, Habits, Grace, Relationships, Health, Abundance, and Death, *Treasury* provides a valuable resource for speakers searching for the seed of a speech, teachers seeking inspiration, or for the reader who simply needs a few words of guidance and comfort.

Whatever your need, you'll find yourself turning to *Treasury* again and again.

The Wisdom of James Allen

5 Classic Works Combined into One
by James Allen
Edited by Andy Zubko
Softcover 384 pp. $7.95 ISBN: 1-889606-00-6

Little is known of James Allen, the mysterious contemplative Englishman who chose a quiet life of voluntary poverty, spiritual self-discipline, and simplicity during the 19th and early 20th centuries. Influenced by the writings of Leo Tolstoy, Allen came to realize that devoting one's life to making money and engaging in frivolous activities is a meaningless way to live.

At age 38, Allen retired with his wife, to a small cottage in southwestern England to devote the remainder of his life to quiet, thoughtful writing.

Allen's best-known book, the spiritual classic *As a Man Thinketh*, has sold steadily over the decades inspiring thousands and thousands of readers to a life of quiet dignity, self-discipline, and contemplation.

This valuable little volume combines four more James Allen books into one exquisite, gift-sized edition. In addition to *As a Man Thinketh*, are: *The Path to Prosperity, The Mastery of Destiny, The Way of Peace,* and *Entering the Kingdom.*

Excerpt from the foreword:

"I looked around upon the world, and saw that it was shadowed by sorrow and scorched by the fierce fires of suffering. And I looked for the cause...And I dreamed of writing books which would help men and women ...to find within themselves the source of all success, the source of all happiness...and now I send forth these books into the world on a mission of healing and blessedness, knowing they cannot fail to reach the homes and hearts of those who are waiting and ready to receive them."

Peace Pilgrim's Wisdom
A Very Simple Guide
Compiled by Cheryl Canfield
Softcover   224 pp. $14   ISBN: 1-884997-11-2

"It is considered the highest level of enlightenment to simply 'walk as you talk'— Peace Pilgrim lived out this message. Indeed, she is my hero."— **Dr. Wayne Dyer**, author of *Your Erroneous Zones* and *Your Sacred Self*

"There is no doubt that she was letting God write the script of her life, every moment of the day." — **Gerald Jampolsky**, author of *Love is Letting Go of Fear*

"I am one of many who have admired and emulated the life and wisdom of Peace Pilgrim. Here is an American saint who transcended all national, religious, or sectarian bonds to communicate love, understanding and integrity. Her life was her teaching."— **Dan Millman**, author of *Way of the Peaceful Warrior*

Peace Pilgrim was an American sage who for 28 years, from 1953 to 1981, walked in faith across North America. Her vow was *"to remain a wanderer until mankind learned the way of peace. Walking until given shelter and fasting until given food."* Penniless, she owned only what she carried, little more than the clothes on her back, a comb and a toothbrush. She walked many thousands of miles as a witness for both inner and outer peace, inspiring people to work for peace in their own lives. Many lives were transformed by her compelling example.

Designed as a study guide, *Peace Pilgrim's Wisdom*, divides her words into 19 sections to help us assimilate these powerful truths into our own lives.

Cheryl Canfield spent much time with Peace Pilgrim and is one of the five compilers of *Peace Pilgrim — Her Life and Work in Her Own Words*, which currently has over 400,000 copies in print.

The Swami Ramdas Trilogy from Blue Dove Press

In Quest of God
The Saga of an Extraordinary Pilgrimage
by Swami Ramdas
Preface by Eknath Easwaran
Foreword by Ram Dass (Richard Alpert)
Softcover   190 pp. $10.95   ISBN: 1-884997-01-5

This is the tale of a remarkable pilgrimage. Walking in a God-intoxicated state of total surrender to the divine will, Swami Ramdas traveled the dusty roads of India as a penniless monk. This narrative, told with a keen wit, contains many inspiring accounts of how his pure love transformed many he encountered who at first behaved harshly toward him.

In the Vision of God Volume 1
The Continuing Saga of an Extraordinary Pilgrimage
by Swami Ramdas
Softcover   288 pp. $14.95   ISBN: 1-884997-03-1

Beginning where *In Quest of God* leaves off, this chronicle of Swami Ramdas' pilgrimage is comparable to such famous classics as *The Way of the Pilgrim* and Brother Lawrence's *The Practice of the Presence of God.*

In the Vision of God Volume 2
The Conclusion to the Saga of an
Extraordinary Pilgrimage
by Swami Ramdas
Softcover   280 pp. $14.95   ISBN: 1-884997-05-8

In this final volume the story of Swami Ramdas' pilgrimage concludes with the end of his wanderings and relates how he settled down in an ashram created for him by his many devotees. This became more than a center for spiritual aspirants, but also a vehicle to help the needs of the local people.

The Lights of Grace
Catalog
from
Blue Dove Press

It is the mission of Blue Dove to make available and promote the messages, lives, and examples of saints and sages of all religions and traditions, as well as other spiritually-oriented works. We do so both by publishing inspirational books and tapes, and distributing the works of other publishers which also provide tools for inner growth.

The *Lights of Grace* catalog is the culmination of our efforts to date. From Saint Teresa of Avila to Milarepa, the Tibetan yogi, we have assembled an inspired collection of spiritual literature at its most diverse and best.

Great saints tend to transcend any single sect, regardless of the path they themselves have chosen. Their perspective is universal. It is our belief that people who have gone beyond the constraints and conditioning of the ego and have realized God, the Self, inner peace, *moksha*—call it what you will—are a tremendous resource for the entire planet. We believe that reading about and studying their lives, messages and examples is of great assistance on our own spiritual path. At Blue Dove, we are committed to contributing to the spiritual unfoldment of all. Blue Dove Press is not affiliated with any particular path, tradition, or religion.

To order contact:

Blue Dove Press
4204 Sorrento Valley Blvd. Suite K
San Diego, CA 92121
Phone: (619)623-3330
FAX: (619)623-3325
Orders: (800)691-1008
E-Mail: bdp@bluedove.com
Website:www.bluedove.com